"Every church library and pastor . . . and a year should not go by without a small group read of this book to equip members of the congregation to support one another on journeys of recovery, emotional well-being, and a healthy spirituality. Barbara Meyers is a courageous and insightful guide to struggles with mental illness, trauma, and substance use. You will find help for your personal healing and wisdom in caring for a family member or friend. Colleagues in psychiatry, psychology, and social work too will find an understanding of spirituality and human vulnerability that honors the importance of faith and hope for our healing and growth. An incredibly informative book!

—Craig Rennebohm, author of *Souls in the Hands of a Tender God: Stories of the Search for Home and Healing on the Streets*

"Barbara Meyers provides a rich tapestry of her lived experience matched with a simple yet compelling framework of practical skills and resources to not only equip but guide every congregation in creating an environment to hold those who need to be held by a community of faith. This must-have resource is accessible and usable to any layperson or faith leader who desires to create a welcoming and inclusive place of worship for those who may experience mental health and substance use challenges."

—Rev. Jermine Alberty, M.Div., Executive Director, Pathways to Promise

"In courageously sharing her own struggles with mental illness, Rev. Barbara Meyers provides encouragement for others to share their stories instead of suffering in silence. *Held: Showing Up for Each Other's Mental Health* provides helpful information, guidance, and study questions to help faith leaders and members of congregations provide a caring and supportive community for the one in five people sitting in the pews dealing with a mental health issue. People of faith can offer the gift of presence without judgment and the reminder that each person has worth and dignity just as they are. Rev. Meyers offers concrete ideas on how living out our beliefs and theology can help our faith communities become beacons of hope for all persons affected by mental illness."

—Rev. Susan Gregg-Schroeder,
Coordinator of Mental Health Ministries

"I find *Held: Showing Up for Each Other's Mental Health* is an excellent guide on how lay persons, especially in a UU congregation, can treat persons with mental health issues in a caring and humane manner. The author reduces the stigma and discrimination of a mental health diagnosis by sharing her own story of severe distress and recovery. She also shows that there is often a spiritual component to the distress and recovery persons go through. Particularly helpful are her suggestions about how to be with a person in distress. In addition to active listening, she points to the value of Emotional CPR."

—Daniel B. Fisher, MD, PhD, President,
National Coalition for Mental Health Recovery

"In *Held*, Barbara Meyers offers a practical, concrete, comprehensive, and authentic guidebook that will be invaluable for faith communities. Based on her own experience and grounded in a solid understanding of all the various aspects of mental illness as well as her own faith journey, this book is a must-read for congregations who want to be communities of support for those who have so often been marginalized by their illness, and for their families. Ending each chapter with discussion questions is an excellent way to make the participants reflect on their own experiences and address their fears and concerns."

> —Nancy Kehoe, RSCJ, PhD, Roman Catholic nun, clinical psychologist, and author of *Wrestling with Our Inner Angels: Faith, Mental Illness and the Journey to Wholeness*

"This book is a gift! Through the power of personal storytelling, scriptural insights, and practical tips, Rev. Meyers teaches us how to show up for each other's mental health so we can experience the healing power of being held in love."

> —Rev. Dr. Sarah Lund, MSW, MDiv, DMin, United Church of Christ Minister for Disabilities and Mental Health Justice

"How come Unitarian Universalist congregations are so good at delivering casseroles and pastoral care to those with trauma or physical illness, but those with mental health are too often left waiting at the door? With that provocative question, Rev. Meyers speaks from her own experience to offer how mental illness deserves not just a medical and therapeutic response, but also a spiritual one that congregations are particularly equipped to offer. Rooting this response in our tradition's Principles of the inherent worth of each person and justice and compassion for all, *Held* helps us see how core congregational practices like kindness, hope, presence, encouragement, and authenticity can help us show up for each other's mental health. I have longed for a book like this to share with my congregation for years and now I can."

—Rev. Nathan Detering, Senior Minister,
Unitarian Universalist Area Church at
First Parish in Sherborn, Massachusetts

HELD

SHOWING UP FOR EACH OTHER'S MENTAL HEALTH

HELD

SHOWING UP FOR EACH OTHER'S MENTAL HEALTH

A GUIDE FOR EVERY MEMBER OF THE CONGREGATION

BARBARA F. MEYERS

Skinner House Books
BOSTON

www.skinnerhouse.org

Printed in the United States

Cover design by Tim Holtz
Text design by Jeff Miller
Author photo by Beckett Gladney

print ISBN: 978-1-55896-859-2
eBook ISBN: 978-1-55896-860-8

6 5 4 3 2 1
24 23 22 21 20

Library of Congress Cataloging-in-Publication Data
Names: Meyers, Barbara F., author.
Title: Held : showing up for each other's mental health / Barbara F. Meyers.
Description: Boston : Skinner House Books, 2020. | Summary: "In Held, community minister and mental health advocate Barbara F. Meyers illustrates how members of liberal religious congregations can be supportive to those living with mental health problems. Meyers addresses the fundamental elements of spiritual support—truth, hope, presence, acceptance, encouragement, authenticity, public witness, pastoral care, and safe places—with stories from real life situations and suggestions for how parishioners can provide and advocate for support in their congregations"—Provided by publisher.
Identifiers: LCCN 2020022237 (print) | LCCN 2020022238 (ebook) | ISBN 9781558968592 (print) | ISBN 9781558968608 (ebook)
Subjects: LCSH: Mental health—Religious aspects. | Unitarian Universalist Association.
Classification: LCC BL65.M45 M49 2020 (print) | LCC BL65.M45 (ebook) | DDC 261.8/322—dc23
LC record available at https://lccn.loc.gov/2020022237
LC ebook record available at https://lccn.loc.gov/2020022238

Thanks to Wayne Arnason, Mark Belletini, Mark Morrison-Reed, Rebecca Parker, and Ken Reeves for permission to reproduce their work.

"Anthem" by Leonard Cohen. Copyright © 1992 by Leonard Cohen, used by permission of The Wylie Agency LLC.

If you or someone you love is struggling with a mental health problem . . .

If you are currently doing well, but are mindful of the fact that you or a loved one or a dear parishioner may someday struggle with a mental health problem . . .

If you know that someone in your religious community is struggling with a mental health problem . . .

This book is dedicated to you, in hopes that you may help change our culture's attitudes about mental health in your congregation and the larger world

Every night and every morn
Some to misery are born;
Every morn and every night
Some are born to sweet delight.

Joy and woe are woven fine,
A clothing for the soul divine.
Under every grief and pine
Runs a joy with silken twine.

It is right it should be so,
We were made for joy and woe;
And, when this we rightly know,
Through the world we safely go.

—Hymn #17, "Every Night and
Every Morn," in *Singing the
Living Tradition.* Words are
drawn from William Blake,
Auguries of Innocence (1863)

A NOTE ON TERMINOLOGY

IN THIS BOOK I use a variety of terms—*mental health issue, mental health crisis, emotional crisis, mental health challenge, mental health difficulty, mental problem, mental health problem, mental disorder,* and *mental illness*—to refer to the circumstances or experiences of people whose mental health has become problematic. The terms *mental disorder* and *mental illness* refer to a condition that has been diagnosed by a mental health professional. The other terms are used interchangeably to refer to any problematic mental health condition, including those that are diagnosed.

I use the term *recovery* from a mental health difficulty to mean a process of change in which people improve their mental health and wellness, live a self-directed life, and strive to live their full potential.[1] It does not necessarily mean the

---

[1] This definition of recovery is from the Substance Abuse and Mental Health Services Administration, "SAMHSA's Working Definition of Recovery," store.samhsa.gov/sites/default/files/d7/priv/pep12-recdef.pdf, 2012.

absence of all symptoms. Thus, we can refer to someone *in recovery* to be *living with* a mental health problem.

Using This Book for Congregational Study

This book can be used as a guide for congregational study. After each chapter, there are a set of questions that can be asked in a group setting. During the discussion, remember not to share names or identifying details about individuals unless they have explicitly given you permission to do so in this setting. A format for the operation of such groups is given in appendix A.

CONTENTS

INTRODUCTION

IN THE COURSE of my ministry to people with mental health issues and their loved ones, a member of a Unitarian Universalist congregation told me the following story. Her daughter was diagnosed with schizophrenia; the condition affected her life every day, and she had been repeatedly hospitalized. When her mother told me this story, her daughter had been in a psychiatric ward for several weeks. The family was endeavoring to visit her every evening, often rushing from work to the hospital, just grabbing from the refrigerator anything that might serve for dinner on the way out of the door.

Meanwhile, her husband had been asked if he could provide a meal for a family in the congregation who had a family member recovering from a serious operation. He agreed, cooked a meal, and delivered it to the family, while skipping a meal himself and rushing with his wife to the psychiatric hospital to visit their daughter. Neither the minister nor anyone in the congregation was visiting her, nor had they been asked to do so.

After a few days, his wife considered this situation and thought, "Wait a minute! Why was he asked to prepare a meal for a family with a hospitalized member, when we are in a similar situation and no one is bringing us meals? Is there a double standard here?"

The answer is yes. There is a double standard.

It is common practice in most Unitarian Universalist faith communities to offer many forms of pastoral care to people and families coping with trauma or physical illness. But all too often mental illness goes unseen and unattended to. Mental illnesses are sometimes called "no-casserole diseases." People don't bring casseroles to homes where someone is hospitalized for mental problems. Discomfort, unexamined assumptions about mental illness, and cultural norms isolate people and families who are in desperate need of community support.

This book is a resource for members of congregations who want to learn how to be more intentionally supportive of people with mental health problems and their loved ones. It emphasizes key elements of such support: kindness, hope, presence, acceptance, encouragement, and authenticity. It also reflects on the spiritual dimensions of mental illness and on what can be done to address mental health issues not only within a congregation but also in the wider society.

Mental illness can range from temporary and situational to chronic and lifelong, from invisible to obvious, mild to severe, inconvenient to debilitating. And it can exact a serious toll on sufferers and their families—emotionally, physically, spiritually, and financially.

According to the National Alliance on Mental Illness (www.nami.org/learn-more/mental-health-by-the-numbers), almost 20 percent of American adults experienced mental illness in 2018, and 4.6 percent experienced serious mental illness. Of adults in the United States, perhaps 0.5 percent live with schizophrenia and 2.8 percent with bipolar disorder. Just over 7 percent had a major depressive episode in 2018, and just over 19 percent have an anxiety disorder. (There are many kinds of anxiety disorders, including post-traumatic stress disorder, obsessive-compulsive disorder, different phobias, and others.) Moreover, nearly half of American adults with an addiction also have a co-occurring mental illness.

So in a congregation of a hundred adults, we can expect that twenty of them will experience a mental illness sometime in a given year, with depression, anxiety, bipolar disorder, and schizophrenia being probable diagnoses. And many more members of the congregation—their family members and dear friends—will also be affected. On any Sunday morning in any Unitarian Universalist community, the pews are filled with people living with mental health issues.

We must acknowledge that financial, cultural, geographic, and personal factors can make it difficult for many people to access both mainstream professional mental health care and alternative therapies (such as acupuncture, art therapy, yoga, and others). As I will discuss later, these difficulties are part of why mental health is a social justice issue.

While professional mental health care is an important part of dealing with mental health issues for many people, it is not enough. Professionals can make diagnoses, prescribe medication, and do psychotherapy, but they don't deal with the whole of a person's life. People with mental illness can have difficulty finding communities that will welcome them and people who will treat them with love. They may be socially isolated even within communities, such as congregations, that are theoretically welcoming.

And mental health professionals rarely offer spiritual support. Mental illness is a spiritual problem as well as a medical and psychiatric one. People living with it can experience existential doubts about selfhood, truth, meaning, love, and agency with particular intensity. But even when their need for spiritual care is recognized, it is often left entirely to the minister and congregational leaders to provide it. It's common for people to believe that only doctors and religious professionals can offer meaningful help to people with mental health problems, and that the best thing others can do is either to just treat them like everyone else or to ignore their difficulties. Indeed, while most people with mental health difficulties don't act or talk in an unusual way, at times some do, and people who find their behaviors off-putting or even frightening may avoid engaging with them. But they and their loved ones need the surrounding, enfolding care of an entire community, not just the attention of a few designated leaders.

Let me be clear: Ministers and congregational leaders can and should develop ministries, programs, and policies to serve their congregants with mental health challenges, and appendix C includes resources to help them do so. But every member of a religious or spiritual community can play a role in helping people to live with and heal from these challenges, as well as in supporting friends and family members who are trying to both help their loved ones and deal with their own stress, grief, fear, despair, and frustration. The goal of this book is to assure readers that it is in their power to be helpful to such people in their congregations, and to teach simple, safe ways of ministering to them and advocating for them that don't require professional training. In fact, I believe that it is everyone's responsibility to be helpful in whatever way we can. We owe it to each other as human beings; we are called to it by our Unitarian Universalist Principles.

This book will illustrate the elements of care and involvement that are important for people with a wide range of mental health challenges and their families in congregational settings. This includes people with severe challenges, such as those involving suicidal thoughts and actions. I will not give medical advice, because that should be done by trained professionals who can assess the situation in person. But the fact that medical treatment should be left to professionals doesn't stop us from offering love and care to people with cancer and their families, and it should not stop us from offering them to people with mental health difficulties.

We're all vulnerable to mental health problems. The majority of people will encounter them at some point in their lives, whether they have such problems themselves or someone in their family or circle of dear friends does. Sometimes emotional reactions to life events can deteriorate into serious mental health problems. For example, grief can become depression, worry can become an anxiety disorder, and the shock of a trauma can become post-traumatic stress disorder (PTSD). So each of us has a personal stake in extending the care that we routinely offer to our fellow community members going through difficulties to community members enduring mental health problems.

In discussing psychiatric disabilities, the UUA website says, "Our goal is to encourage you to be involved with a person rather than to be concerned with a diagnostic label. As Unitarian Universalists, we believe in the inherent worth and dignity of every person, and one of the most effective ways we can act on that principle is to treat people as individuals. Each of us is more than the sum of the labels that society may place on us" (www.uua.org/accessibility/psychiatric). This book shares that goal. I encourage you to reflect on the sacredness of every individual, no matter what their diagnosis may be. We need to equip ourselves to understand what people dealing with mental health challenges are experiencing and meet them where they are on their life journey, as their companions and friends. We need to learn from them and let our lives be enriched by being with them. We need to see them through a lens of meaning, value, and beauty.

——————— DISCUSSION QUESTIONS ———————

1. Have you ever had a congregation member bring a meal or perform another service for you when you were in need?

2. Have you ever brought a meal or performed some other service for someone else in your congregation?

3. If people in your congregation have mental health crises, do other congregation members visit them in the psychiatric ward or deliver meals to their home? If not, why not?

4. Do you agree that lay members of congregations can provide support to people with mental health difficulties? Does the prospect frighten or worry you?

MY JOURNEY

You shall know the truth,
and the truth shall set you free.
—John 8:32

I HAVE MINISTERED to many people with mental health difficulties, their family members, and their congregations. Denominationally, I helped to establish the Accessibility and Inclusion Ministry (AIM), a joint program of EqUUal Access (www.equualaccess.org/aim-program) and the UUA that guides congregations to deepen their understanding of disability, including mental health disability, and to be welcoming and inclusive of all. I also helped establish and lead the Unitarian Universalist Mental Health Network. And I am someone who has been there; my calling to this ministry has been strongly influenced by my own experience with mental health issues. I know firsthand the impact that a community of faith can have, and I hope that by speaking openly about my experience I can help dispel the shame that many feel around the topic.

In October 1978 I suffered a severe postpartum depression, for which I was hospitalized. Being in the psychiatric ward of our local hospital was very disturbing for me. I didn't want to accept that I could be like any of "those people," but there I was. Eventually I was able to return to my job and my life, but for years I remained unhappy. The experience left me with deep feelings of self-hate and worthlessness. This was in spite of having a good job, a wonderful and supportive home and family, and good mental health care. I was afraid of having to go back to the psychiatric ward and especially of experiencing psychosis, which I had seen in other patients. It was the worst outcome I could imagine.

These feelings of worthlessness and shame lasted for eight years. I was hyper-sensitive to criticism, believing that it validated my lack of self-worth. Finally, in April 1986, I decided that I didn't want to live like that anymore, and entered into a deeper exploration with my psychiatrist to understand what was behind my unhappiness and try to change it.

After we had been working for some weeks, my psychiatrist asked me if I did anything spiritually for myself. I said I didn't. I had grown up in a nondenominational Protestant church, where I had attended every Sunday and been involved with the youth group. After I went to college, however, my involvement ended.

My psychiatrist asked me if I would like to learn how to meditate, because many people find meditation to be very helpful. My first thought was "You have to be kidding! Sitting around doing nothing?" My whole life had been focused on doing, doing, and more doing. But I agreed to try it, because I had promised myself I would try anything that he suggested might help. Still, I didn't immediately begin meditating. Instead, I read a book he gave me that explained his meditation technique. The book said that God was within, meditation brought us in contact with that God, and wonderful things were possible when you knew God. I hadn't had any spiritual practice for nearly twenty years, and the religion that I had grown up with hadn't taught me that God was within. When I did sit and try to meditate, just for a few minutes at first, this was literally the only time in my day that was calm and peaceful, when I wasn't rushing to do one thing or another.

Not too long after this, I found myself spontaneously happy. I went back to my psychiatrist and told him, "I don't know where it came from, but I'm happy!" I'll never forget what he said. He pointed at me and said, "It came from *you.*" This was contrary to everything I'd thought before, and yet, to my own surprise, I immediately believed it. Happiness comes from within, I now knew. Holiness comes from within. Such beliefs had been foreign to me before, and I was amazed that I could change such fundamental beliefs so quickly. If my psychiatrist was similarly surprised, he didn't mention it to me.

Not long after this, in an important work meeting, I saw halos above the heads of some of the lowest-ranking people in the room: secretaries and underlings. I instantly understood this as a vision from God, showing me an important truth about the world. It wasn't immediately clear to me exactly what this important truth was, but I knew I was being shown some sacred truth. Much later I understood it as showing me that the truly significant people in life are the ones who serve. The experience elated me. I told my psychiatrist that I was cured and didn't need to see him again. And since I was cured, I stopped taking my psychotropic medication cold turkey—not a wise thing to do.

In fact, I was manic, although I didn't know that at the time. It isn't always possible to tell the difference between mania and spiritual exhilaration. The best way I have discovered to distinguish them is by what happens next: whether the effect of the feeling is life enhancing and holy or ultimately destructive.

About a week after I ecstatically bid farewell to my psychiatrist and stopped taking my medication, I began to get the clear feeling that I was going to die. I became increasingly upset as my certainty became stronger and stronger. I would wake in the early hours of the morning, frightened after having dreamed I was dying. Finally, one day at work I became convinced that I would die that day. I shared these thoughts with a friend, who became alarmed when he couldn't reason with me, and he called my husband. They tried to get me to call my psychiatrist, but I refused because, in my muddled logic, doing so would mean admitting I wasn't cured. My husband and my friend took me to the psychiatric hospital, where I was involuntarily committed. I was smiling broadly as I went in, believing that I had died, was entering heaven, and would soon be reborn, just like the other patients. When my family visited me, I thought they were visiting my grave. I wouldn't talk to anyone because I believed I was dead and in a tomb, and dead people don't talk. I was psychotic and almost catatonic.

I still remember everyone who visited me during my two psychiatric hospitalizations, even though they were more than thirty and forty years ago. I don't remember what they said or what we did together, but it wasn't anything particularly profound. Some visits were probably awkward or uncomfortable for the visitor; I remember my father had a pained expression when he came. But he was there. It was the presence of my visitors that spoke volumes to me. It told me that I was worth visiting, that they still cared for me, that I wouldn't be shunned even if I felt like shunning myself. I remember every phone call, every card, every gift.

I was hospitalized for three weeks, although I gradually spent more and more of each day at home with my family, returning at night to the hospital. Over time I regained my mental stability and my sense of self; I felt that I was returning to some form of life. Through all of this, I had regular sessions with my psychiatrist. He was encouraging and positive, but also realistic, and he challenged me when I needed to be challenged. His challenges didn't wound me; I took them as constructive. Coming out of this experience, I found that criticisms from others didn't bother me as they had before. The soul I thought I had lost was still there, healthier than it had ever been.

1. Do you agree that speaking openly about one's experience of mental health difficulties can help dispel the shame that many feel about it?

2. Why do you think that hospital visits can be important to psychiatric inpatients?

3. Not everyone has access to good psychiatric care and a supportive living environment. Do you know anyone who struggles to get adequate mental health care? Do you see access to such care as a social justice issue? (Do not share names or identifying details unless the person you are thinking of has explicitly given you permission to do so in this setting.)

SPIRITUAL IMPLICATIONS
OF MENTAL ILLNESS

Ring the bells that still can ring
Forget your perfect offering
There is a crack, a crack in everything
That's how the light gets in.
—Leonard Cohen, "Anthem"

MENTAL ILLNESS is a spiritual problem as well as a psychiatric one. When people living with it experience existential doubts, they may ask questions like "Why is this happening to me?" or ". . . to my loved one?" These are spiritual as well as practical questions. Lack of an answer can undermine someone's faith in the divine or their belief in justice. Seeking answers to these questions involves a search for truth and meaning, such as we affirm in our fourth Unitarian Universalist Principle. Because people ask these questions at a time of deep turmoil, the spiritual lessons learned through seeking their answers can have a profound impact on a person's life.

Spiritual Awakenings

After I recovered from the acute phase of my second bout of mental illness, I was a changed person. I emerged not damaged but more whole than I had been, and with greater clarity about what was important to me and what I needed in my life. I didn't care as much about many of the things that I had previously valued: status, possessions, the good regard of others. I started attending church for the first time in nearly twenty years and for the first time let spiritual ideas take an important role in my life. I initially chose a Unitarian Universalist congregation because the word *universalist* seemed to match my new way of looking at the world. The church was a very important part of my recovery. I also learned how to weave, which remains my main form of creative artistic expression and a spiritual practice. I became a more complete person.

My psychological and spiritual rebirth has been an ongoing journey. I have established regular spiritual practices, and I have learned to value my nurturing, creative side. A short period as a faculty member at National Hispanic University, helping with administrative issues and teaching computer science, was an important step. I was there to be as helpful as I could to the administration and students, without expecting any reward or promotion for myself. It taught me the blessings that come from selfless service. This experience led me to help start a Unitarian Universalist congregation in my hometown and then start a group in that congregation to help others with mental health difficulties. That in turn led me to change my career and enter seminary with the goal of helping people who, like me, faced mental challenges. Compared to who I was before I began psychotherapy, I have definitely been reborn.

I could not have predicted such an outcome during my first hospitalization in a psychiatric ward. In the ward I saw people who were hallucinating: seeing things that others didn't see and hearing things that others didn't hear. Sometimes they were talking to or shouting at voices that no one else heard. I hadn't seen people who were actively psychotic before, and they frightened me. It never occurred to me that someday I might find a way to see the divine within each of these people and to prefer being with them, in their unpretentious authenticity, to being with more mentally healthy people. But that is where I have arrived.

It may seem impossible to believe that anything good can come out of an illness so severe that it endangers a person's ability to function in the world. Serious mental illness can be a nightmarish experience for both sufferers and their families. It can involve repeated hospitalization and even incarceration. It can lead to significant family dissension. It can threaten the sufferer's life. But I have come to believe that people can recover and that life after the crisis can be richer than before it. Contrary to what some might expect, my second mental health crisis was spiritually regenerative. Recovery from it was more than a return to a previous state. It brought growth and transformation so that I could integrate the lessons of the crisis into a deeper understanding and worldview.

People who are suffering or witnessing the depths of a mental health crisis may find it difficult to believe that such a crisis can bring an authentic spiritual awakening. The key to understanding this possibility may be that such a crisis does not arise out of nowhere. Typically it is preceded by a long period of struggling with a mental health problem, often undiagnosed and untreated. The crisis can precipitate seeking and finding appropriate care and thus mark the beginning of a path toward not only recovery but a previously unexperienced wholeness. In my own case, my first experience of mental illness was deeply disturbing to me, leaving me in a fragile state, sensitive to criticism. But my second experience left me much stronger and more grounded.

Even I recognize this only in retrospect; it was not clear to me at the time of my own crisis. The spiritual awakening involved in my recovery came through my discovery of inner strength and resources and through the love and support of others. Through patience, forgiveness, self-compassion, gratitude, and trust, I learned that even impossible-seeming hopes can be realized.

I no longer believe that acute psychosis is the worst thing that could happen to me. I've been through it and, now that I've recovered, found it actually beneficial. While I know very well that psychosis and other acute mental illnesses can be horrific for the person experiencing them, for me it opened the door to a new way of conceiving of myself and my purpose and meaning. In the end, it brought me peace.

Also, I have come to believe that psychosis can sometimes have a psychological truth that is deeper than the literal truth. It is true in the way that dreams are true. It wasn't true that I was physically dying or that I was dead. That belief was unquestionably harmful to me, and I needed help to overcome it. But it was true that my old, limited view of myself—that I had to be perfect, that only rationality mattered, that I cared about other people's opinions of me—was dying. I've subsequently learned that in psychoanalytic terms, such a loss of self-image is sometimes called the "death of the ego." Recovery for me meant becoming able to integrate psychological truths into my understanding of the world without confusing them with literal, factual reality. Now, when speaking to someone who is psychotic, I try to think of how their experience might be psychologically true and potentially helpful to them in the long run.

When I left the hospital for the second time, I realized that something spiritual had happened to me. It is not uncommon for the symptoms of some mental disorders to resemble experiences involved in spiritual awakening. Such experiences have helped shape the religious landscape throughout human history; the prophets and patriarchs of most religious traditions saw visions and heard voices, and they are central to many indigenous shamanic traditions. Jesus, the Apostle Paul, George Fox (founder of the Quakers), the prophet Ezekiel, Saint Teresa, and Martin Luther all had experiences that might be described as mental health crises today, as did the Prophet Mohammed and many Hindu mystics. They emerged from their experiences with new insights and more comprehensive understandings, ideas that eventually led them to their prophetic work.[2]

A religious community can help individuals and families affected by mental health crises by providing a place to try to articulate spiritual truths, as distinct from literal truths, and give them healthy expression. Our Fourth Principle, in which we affirm a free and responsible search for truth and meaning, especially helps with this. We know that one person's truth and meaning may not be the same as another's and that our truths may change, we may find new meanings, as the circumstances of our lives evolve. The Fourth Principle encourages us to be authentic in our beliefs, and authenticity is important for mental health.[3]

---

[2] Anton T. Boisen, *The Exploration of the Inner World: A Study of Mental Disorder and Religious Experience* (Philadelphia: University of Pennsylvania Press, 1936). For a more modern exploration of the topic, see Emma Bragdon, *The Call of Spiritual Emergency: From Personal Crisis to Personal Transformation*, 2nd ed. (Woodstock, VT: Lightening Up Press, 2013). Bragdon trains people in integrative mental health and spiritual emergence coaching; for more information, see Integrative Mental Health For You (imhu.org).

[3] On the relationship between authenticity and mental health, see D. Grijak, "Authenticity as a Predictor of Mental Health," *Klinička Psihologija* 10, nos. 1–2 (2017): 23–34; and Jennifer L. Bryan, Zachary G. Baker, and Reese Y. W. Tou, "Prevent the Blue, Be True to You: Authenticity Buffers the Negative Impact of Loneliness on Alcohol-Related Problems, Physical Symptoms, and Depressive and Anxiety Symptoms," *Journal of Health Psychology* 22, no. 5 (2017): 605–16.

I find it useful here to distinguish between *spirituality* and *religion*. Here are helpful definitions I have adapted from several sources:[4]

- **Spirituality** is a complex and multidimensional part of the human experience: our inner belief system. It helps individuals search for the meaning and purpose of life, and it helps them experience hope, love, inner peace, comfort, and support.
- **Religion** is an organized belief system or set of guiding principles to which an individual adheres and which involves observance of particular rituals and practices. It can be understood as the search for significance that occurs within the context of established institutions that are designed to facilitate spirituality.

Many people find spirituality through religion; however, some people find spirituality through nature, music, the

---

[4] Joint Commission on Accreditation of Healthcare Organizations, "Evaluating Your Spiritual Assessment Process," *The Source* 3, no. 2 (2005): 6–7; Gowri Anandarajah and Ellen Hight, "Spirituality and Medical Practice: Using the HOPE Questions as a Practical Tool for Spiritual Assessment," *American Family Physician* 63, no. 1 (2001): 81–89; Substance Abuse and Mental Health Services Administration, "Understanding and Building on Culture and Spirituality in Recovery-Oriented Practice," webinar with Rev. Laura L. Mancuso, Dolores Subia BigFoot, and Gladys Christian, April 4, 2012, storiesfromtheroad.typepad.com/blog/2014/06/samhsa-webinar-on -spirituality.html; and Pargament, K. I., et al., "Envisioning an integrative paradigm for the psychology of religion and spirituality." In APA *Handbook of Psychology, Religion, and Spirituality (Vol. 1): Context, Theory, and Research*: 3–19. American Psychological Association. doi.org/10.1037/14045-001.

arts, the quest for scientific truth, or a set of values and principles.

There are people who have experienced religion as helpful to their mental health. Some others have experienced it as harmful. This book is intended to help members of religious communities make their communities safe and supportive places for mental health, so it is important to understand what kinds of religious practices have been harmful. We must not fall into those practices, and even when we avoid them, we must remember that people may come to our congregations carrying anxieties about religion and sensitive to even echoes or suggestions of them.

At its origin, psychoanalysis was hostile to religion.[5] Those who feel that religion doesn't help, and may harm, mental health argue that it has the potential to

- generate unhealthy levels of guilt,
- promote self-denigration and low self-esteem by devaluing human nature,
- establish a foundation for the unhealthy repression of anger,

---

[5] Sigmund Freud, *The Future of an Illusion*, originally published in 1927. Freud's thesis is that religion is a childish illusion. The psychologist Eric Fromm writes that Freud "sees in the belief in God a fixation to the longing for an all-protecting father figure, an expression of a wish to be helped and saved, when in reality man can, if not save himself, at least help himself, only by waking up from childish illusions and by using his own strength, his reason and skills" (*Sigmund Freud's Mission: An Analysis of His Personality and Influence* [New York: Harper and Row, 1959], 95).

- create anxiety and fear through belief in punishment (e.g., in hell) for "evil" ways,
- impede self-direction and a sense of internal control,
- foster dependency, conformity, and overreliance on external forces,
- inhibit the expression of sexual feelings,
- encourage black-and-white views of the world, such that all are either "saints" or "sinners,"
- instill paranoia concerning evil forces that threaten one's integrity, and
- interfere with rational and critical thought.[6]

In recent years, however, mental health professionals have increasingly realized that spirituality and religion can sometimes be helpful to recovery. People heal in relationship to other people, and acceptance in a community where their presence is honored and where they can be honest about the mental health challenges they face is central to recovery and to living with their situation.

Dimensions of Wellness

The United States Department of Health and Human Services' Substance Abuse and Mental Health Services Agency (SAMHSA) has developed a model showing eight dimensions

---

[6] John F. Schumaker, introduction to *Religion and Mental Health* (New York: Oxford University Press, 1992), 3–4.

of wellness: spiritual, emotional, social, occupational, financial, environmental, physical, and intellectual.[7] Religion and the religious community can play an important role in each.

- **Spiritual dimension.** Many people find that spirituality can bring a sense of purpose and meaning into their life. Living life according to deeply held values and beliefs, and acting in concert with the divine as you feel it, can lessen anxiety and stress. A congregation can spiritually support those who are struggling by encouraging and supporting them in their search for truth and meaning. Some resources for doing this are included in the UUA's Tapestry of Faith programs (www.uua.org/re/tapestry/adults).
- **Emotional dimension.** Members of a congregation can help to foster a troubled person's hope, self-esteem, and peace of mind by encouraging them to persevere, appreciating their efforts in the congregation, being present with them, and praying with them. For example, if someone is facing a recurrence of a familiar difficulty, it might be useful to ask them, "What helped you when you went through this before?"
- **Social dimension.** When members of a congregation build relationships with one another, all can feel more accepted and know that they can help others in

---

[7] See, for instance, SAMHSA, "What Individuals in Recovery Need to Know about Wellness," store.samhsa.gov/sites/default/files/d7/priv/sma16-4950.pdf, 2016.

addition to being helped themselves. Participating in potluck dinners and small group ministry made me feel that I belonged and that my fellow congregants were my dear companions on my life journey.

- **Occupational dimension.** In spiritual communities, people can learn to identify and deliver their gifts. Often they can use these gifts to creatively enhance worship and other congregational activities. In my first Unitarian Universalist congregation, I helped make a quilt depicting special events in the church's history. In another project, I created a panel for the NAMES Project Memorial Quilt honoring people the minister knew who had died of AIDS. The congregation's appreciation of my skills did wonders for my self-esteem. Inviting people to play a role in a social justice project is another way of connecting them with something larger than themselves and helping them to see that they can play a part in making the world a better place. Any activity that helps a person see that their life matters is valuable.

- **Financial dimension.** Members of congregations can assist those in financial difficulty by providing occasional meals and short-term housing. For more lasting impact, they can help people access food aid and low-income housing.

- **Environmental dimension.** Many congregations find ways of connecting with and honoring nature. Many people with mental health difficulties find that being

in a natural setting can be helpful, changing their sur-
roundings and allowing respite from what is troubling
them.

- **Physical dimension.** If a person is having difficulty
with medication, members of their congregation can
encourage them to work with their doctors to find a
more effective regimen. If they need more exercise,
people can offer to go on walks or bike rides with them.

- **Intellectual dimension.** Congregations often have
adult education programs that offer opportunities for
both spiritual learning and the exercise of reason.
Classes and small group ministry programs could
include such topics as worship, sacred texts, evolution,
writing, mindfulness, and poetry. Curricula, resources,
and support for these programs can be found on the
UUA website (www.uua.org/re/adults).

Sometimes people with mental health difficulties—or
their family members—think that all they need to do to
recover is to take medication and get psychotherapy if they
can. But this is not enough. Medication is very important
for some people, but it is only one part of one of the eight
dimensions of wellness. The central idea of the SAMHSA
model is that a person's recovery involves all of these dimensions of their lives, not just one or two. Because the religious
community can play an important role in all of them, acceptance and engagement in such a community can be important parts of recovery.

Kenneth Pargament writes that some people enter psycho-therapy

> presenting problems attributable in one way or another to that lost sense of the sacred, such as the depression that grows out of spiritual emptiness, the anxiety that accompanies the feeling of life being lived inauthentically, and the pursuit of false gods such as consumerism, workaholism, narcissism, nihilism, hedonism, and alcoholism—those destructive "isms" of our times. . . .
>
> The list of potential false gods seems endless: drugs, alcohol, sex, anger, anxiety, physical objects, money, people, fame, power, relationships and so on. . . . False gods are problematic not because they are false in the ontological sense, . . . but because they are incapable of holding the sacred. They also become problematic when people approach them as idols, confusing symbols of the divine with the divine itself. The end result is a life dedicated to gods that diminish rather than enrich human experience.[8]

I agree with Pargament that mental health struggles are linked to spiritual emptiness, but I think that for some people, his cause and effect might be flipped. For some, it might

---

[8] Kenneth Pargament, *Spiritually Integrated Psychotherapy: Understanding and Addressing the Sacred* (New York: Guilford Press, 2011), 246, 279.

be that the symptoms of spiritual emptiness are the spiritual consequences of a person's mental illness.

John Schumaker explains that religion can benefit mental health by

- offering order and structure in a sometimes chaotic world, reducing anxiety,
- offering hope, meaning, and purpose, and thus a sense of emotional well-being,
- providing reassurance, enabling one to withstand suffering and pain,
- offering afterlife beliefs, helping to solve the problem of mortality,
- offering moral guidelines for life to serve self and others,
- offering a social identity, acceptance, and belonging, and
- providing cathartic release through participation in ritual.[9]

Four of our Unitarian Universalist Principles are of particular importance to those struggling with their mental health:

- **First: The inherent worth and dignity of every person.** A person with a mental health difficulty can sometimes doubt their own worth. This Principle assures them that we believe all people have worth. I believe

---

[9] Schumaker, introduction to *Religion and Mental Health*, 3.

that within each person is a spark of divinity, and when I am with a person with a mental problem, I concentrate on seeing that spark within them.

- **Second: Justice, equity, and compassion in human relations.** The word *compassion* comes from the Latin for "suffer with," and the ability to suffer with another is the foundation of much mental health support. The spiritual love that we have for our fellow human beings is the basis for compassion.

- **Third: Acceptance of one another and encouragement to spiritual growth in our congregations.** To live and thrive, people need a safe and caring place in which they are accepted and encouraged to grow. This is especially true for those who are trying to live with mental health challenges. I see the divine between people, as well as within each person, and for me this Principle shows the importance of spiritual relationship within a religious community.

- **Fourth: A free and responsible search for truth and meaning.** This Principle can have particular resonance for people who are building up their mental world after a crisis of depression or delusion. It encourages them to create a spiritual structure that works for them, with the support of a religious community.

Many people can find hope in the faith that they are being held by someone or something larger than themselves. This might be God, the human spirit, or the universe. This faith is at the core of many addiction recovery programs, including twelve-step programs. It can allow them to surrender to an entity that receives them unconditionally, to know that they do not suffer alone, and to hope that things can get better. People need spiritual community not just because they're lonely. They need to be included in a congregation's spiritual development opportunities, both formal and informal: for instance, both the sermon and conversations about it in coffee hour afterward.

Spiritual Practice

While many treatments, practices, and lifestyle changes can aid in recovery from mental health problems, studies have shown that one of the most important is spirituality. Spiritual practice is one of the primary coping mechanisms for people with such problems.[10] The kinds of spiritual practices are many: traditional prayer, meditation, ritual, and others. Rev. Kathleen McTigue, the director of the Unitarian Universalist College of Social Justice, explains,

> Despite their many variations, three essential threads weave through all spiritual practices: intention, atten-

---

[10] National Mental Health Consumers' Self-Help Clearinghouse, "Report from Recovery Plank," First National Summit of Mental Health Consumers and Survivors, Portland, Oregon, August 26–29, 1999, www.mhselfhelp.org/the-first-national-summit; and David Lukoff and Laura L. Mancuso, *Survey of Individuals Receiving Mental Health Services and Their Families* (Sacramento: California Mental Health and Spirituality Initiative, 2010).

tion, and repetition. Intention is the deliberate engagement of our will, in a practice that nurtures a sense of connection to something bigger than ourselves. Attention means we exist only in the present moment: We practice quieting the incessant chatter of our minds in order to receive one moment at a time with openness, curiosity, and a willingness to be with what is. Repetition allows our centering activity to form part of the rhythm of our day, and . . . helps us hone qualities like awareness, patience, and compassion.[11]

Spiritual practice lifts a person's body and mind out of the everyday world, relieving their mental pain, even if only for a short while. Such practice is a healthier coping strategy than substance abuse or denial, and it's one that the person can design for themselves and always have available to them. In a 2010 survey conducted by the California Mental Health and Spirituality Initiative, many people said that prayer or another spiritual practice had been the single most helpful thing for them in dealing with a mental health crisis, whether their own or a family member's, and it had been helpful both at the time of crisis and later, over time.[12] Indeed, a mental health crisis can bring a spiritual transformation that might not be evident at first. For me, the

---

[11] Kathleen McTigue, "Drawing on the Deep Waters: Contemplative Practice in Justice-Making," in *Justice on Earth: People of Faith Working at the Intersections of Race, Class, and the Environment*, ed. Manish Mishra-Marzetti and Jennifer Nordstrom (Boston: Skinner House Books, 2018), 68.
[12] Lukoff and Mancuso, *Survey*.

spiritual experience of being unconditionally loved by God, just the way that I am, was fundamental to my recovery. Reminding myself of God's love and visualizing myself as being held by God, even at my lowest point, was a practice that grounded me and continues to ground me.

As members of a congregation, we can encourage and help people to find a spiritual practice that is helpful to them. For some, this might mean simply participating in Sunday services; for others it may require exploration and creativity. We might do this one-on-one or as part of a group activity, a retreat, or a congregational spiritual exploration program.

———————— DISCUSSION QUESTIONS ————————

1. Have you known someone who has had a spiritual awakening as part of a mental health crisis? If so, can you explain what happened? How might your congregation honor these kinds of experiences?

2. Do you agree with the definitions of *spirituality* and *religion* and the relationship between them that are given in this chapter? If not, how would you define them?

3. Do you agree that Unitarian Universalist Principles are beneficial to mental health? If so, where does our practice of them sometimes fall short?

4. Do you agree that psychological truth can be different from literal truth? Have you ever felt a psychological truth yourself that was not literally true?

5. What spiritual practices have been helpful to you at times of emotional crisis?

ONE-ON-ONE SUPPORT

The deepest act of love is not help or service; it is immediate, attentive presence.

—Gerald May, MD

THE NEXT TIME that you hear of a family who has a loved one in a psychiatric hospital, I encourage you to ask them what they need. Or, better yet—but only if you have the person's permission—talk to your congregation's pastoral care team. They are uniquely qualified to give spiritual support that that person and their family may not receive anywhere else and that is so important to people coping with a mental health challenge.

Dr. Mark Ragins is a staff psychiatrist at The Village, an integrated service agency in Long Beach, California, that is renowned for its success in treating difficult psychiatric cases, often involving homelessness, schizophrenia, and substance abuse. He says,

> When I ask psychiatric patients who have done well what I did that was helpful to them . . . they almost always recount some moment of human connectedness: "It was when you hugged me and I could tell you knew how much it pained me to have my child taken away." "It was when you believed in me, when I couldn't believe in myself." "It was when you lent me $5.00 even though you're not supposed to." "It was when you drove me home from the hospital in your car even though I was smelly." "It was when I knew you really cared and wouldn't give up on me."[13]

In other words, it was when they were the recipient of an act of human kindness or when someone believed in them. These moments are what help in healing.

Here is where the faith community comes in. People of faith are experts in human kindness. We can believe in people. We can see something inside them that they aren't able to see themselves. We can give acceptance and love even when an illness is untreated or a person feels hopeless. And these may be central factors in recovery.

I know this to be true for me. When I started attending a Unitarian Universalist church in Hayward, California, shortly after being released from a psychiatric hospital, I didn't tell anyone but the minister about my hospitalization.

---

[13] Mark Ragins, "Up Close and Personal: A Plea for Emotional Connection with Patients," 2004, http://static1.1.sqspcdn.com/static/f/1084149/1547556 9/1323193984247/&break;56UpCloseandPersonal.pdf.

The people in the church showed me many kindnesses: they involved me in church projects like a group quilt, they complimented the bread I baked for coffee hour, they comforted me when my mother-in-law died, they were interested in my ideas. In other words, they treated me as a person with inherent worth and dignity; they treated me with compassion; and they offered me ways to search for truth and meaning. Which is to say: They treated me in accordance with the Unitarian Universalist Principles.

The congregation taught me to believe that each person is inherently worthy. Learning this, I came to understand that even people who have been hospitalized for psychiatric problems are all God's children.

Even me.

Even me.

That lesson changed the course of my life, and I am eternally grateful.

Presence

Sometimes we avoid trying to help someone with mental health problems because we don't know what to do or say. We worry that we're not qualified to help and might make the situation worse. But the most powerful thing we can do is the easiest thing. Just be present. Just listen. Sometimes that's all it takes to make a difference.

Once, during my ministerial internship, a woman I'll call Clara came up to me during the hustle and bustle before the Sunday service. I knew that Clara struggled with anxiety; now, in great distress, she told me how anxious she was and that she didn't know what to do. She was frantic, and I didn't know what I could do for her. At a loss, I suggested that we get out of the busy hallway and go together to a nearby empty room. I sat with her there, holding her hand in silence, and thinking, "What can I do? What can I say? I don't know what to do. . . ." After a couple of minutes, she said to me, "I feel so much better just sitting here with you." I was amazed to realize that just by being present with Clara, caring about her, I had helped her; that my presence, in and of itself, was a gift. And that her acknowledging it was a gift to me.

I have also learned this lesson in my work as a community minister in a mental health center. One day a long-time client I will call Sally was having a very hard time. As I spoke with her, it seemed to me that her condition was deteriorating rapidly. I knew that she had been hospitalized several times before and found help there, so I asked her if she thought she needed to go to the hospital again, and she said yes. I took her to the hospital and sat with her in the waiting room, helping her to fill out the admission forms and holding her hand until she was admitted. A few weeks later, after she was discharged, she told me that she wanted to tell me something. She said, "I want you to know that the fact that you took me to the hospital and sat there helping me to fill out the forms and waiting with me was so important to me. Just thinking about what you did for me sometimes helps me to get through the day." What a gift to receive from her! I will always treasure it.

It is not only ministers who can help in this way. A congregant who notices that a person's situation is deteriorating can offer to help them contact their doctor, or even take them to the hospital and stay with them until they are safely in care. It is the help and companionship, the presence, that make the difference.

I will always be grateful to Clara and Sally for teaching me the importance of presence, of caring personal attention to someone in distress. I was present with Clara and Sally as things in their lives were breaking down, as they were filled with anxiety, and as they struggled with bureaucracy. And my presence did not only help them. It also helped me in my search for truth and meaning, in forming my own theology.

My ministerial internship was half parish based and half community based. I worked both at a large downtown church and in the streets of a nearby impoverished community. I learned then, and continue to learn, that although the people in more privileged environments are more likely to have their needs met, both those in the church and those in the streets struggle with many of the same human needs, needs that are often exacerbated by mental health challenges. And I learned that presence is a gift that helps people cope with these challenges. Just being there is as important as anything I could do. As the Chinese philosopher and writer Lao Tzu is reputed to have said, "The way to do is to be."

Another example of the power of presence in situations involving mental illness comes from a personal communication with Rev. Mark Belletini:

> One day a member of a congregation called his minister at 11 p.m. and said, "Would you do me a favor?" "What do you want?" the minister inquired, surprised by the call. "Would you come sit on my wife?" The minister was totally baffled and inquired further. It turned out that the man's wife had gone off the medicine she had been taking that treated her bipolar disorder, and she was tearing the house apart. He didn't know how to restrain her in this condition, except to sit on her, and he was a large man and reasoned that doing so might hurt her. The minister decided to go over to their house and be present as a quiet and calming presence, simply calling her by her name, over and over. And it worked. She eventually took her medication and after an hour fell asleep. It's a dramatic story in some respects, but it's more common than some might imagine.

Family members need support when they are trying to cope with a loved one's mental health crisis. Even more important than what the minister did may have been the simple fact that he was there, that the husband did not have to go through this difficult experience with his wife alone.

Unitarian Universalism encourages us to engage in a free and responsible search for truth and meaning. My own experience has led me to see the divine in three places: within each human being, between human beings, and beyond human beings. When two people are together and attentive to each other, there is something sacred between them, something more than they have separately. When I sat with Clara and with Sally, neither of us had any idea how to address their problems. Yet, when we were simply together, without even saying anything, serenity appeared as an unexpected gift. I'm reminded of Jesus saying, "Where two or three are gathered in my name, there am I in the midst of them" (Matthew 18:20), and I have come to see the sacred space and connection between people as an important part of my theology.

Active Listening

It can be difficult for someone in a mental health crisis to be listened to or taken seriously. People often don't want—or feel they don't know how—to talk to them, and when they do engage they often assume that the person will not make sense and can't be reasoned with. Many people with mental illness are also members of other marginalized communities and are doubly shunned. For many mentally ill people, it is a rare experience simply to be heard and attended to rather than avoided or dismissed.

Active listening is an effective way to be present with anyone, including someone experiencing a mental health problem. I offer here some guidelines adapted with permission from a workshop that Rev. Dr. Ken Reeves, a Unitarian Universalist minister and clinical psychologist, offered at Mission Peak Unitarian Universalist Congregation:

- Look at and focus on the other person. They are giving you a gift of vulnerability. Stand in awe of their courage as they let you in.
- Begin the conversation with a broad opening statement, allowing the other person to determine what will be discussed.
- Listen without judgment to what the person is trying to convey. Attend to words, feelings, and nonverbal communication, especially when there is a contradiction between their body language and their words.
- As they speak, respond in a way that communicates you understand their message.
  - Respond in the moment, rather than saving up everything you might say for a long speech later.
  - Acknowledge the person's feelings by restating, reflecting, or paraphrasing them: "I hear you saying that you feel scared"; "You feel you can't go on."
  - Validate their feelings: "Yes, it's confusing to receive so many different opinions."
  - If you accidentally talked over them, undo and refocus: "I think I cut you off earlier when you were

talking about your worries. Did you have more you wanted to say about that?"

- Encourage them to tell their story.
  - Ask for details: "What happened then?" "What was your father like?"
  - Clarify what you have heard: "Are you saying that it's difficult to talk with your partner?" "Sounds like you're dealing with a nasty boss."
  - When hearing a vague generalization, ask for an example: "When was the last time that happened?"
- Reflect back to them what you believe to be the main idea they have conveyed.
- Allow yourself to express your natural responses.
  - Respond in words: "I am so sorry"; "How do you feel?"; "How are you handling this?"
  - Respond in actions: hold their hand, hug them, offer tissues, cry yourself.
- It is all right to ask the person to go deeper: "What is the worst aspect of this?"; "What else do you feel?"; "What are the losses you face?"
- Be specific. General statements like "You're too nervous" are not useful.
- Describe rather than evaluate. It's better to describe how you feel about something the person has said than to put a label on it.
- Be brief. Keep yourself to a sentence or two if possible.
- Ask, "What has been helpful in the past?"

- Recognize that you do not need to control the other person's emotions.
- Share your observations or perceptions: "I imagine you are in great pain"; "You seem to be struggling with anger."
- Ask, "What can I do for you?" It may be helpful to suggest possibilities:
  - Ongoing emotional support
  - Logistical help, such as bringing meals, doing shopping or home or pet care, providing transportation
  - Social support, such as arranging visits from congregation members

There are also actions and words that take away from your attentive presence to the other person. Here are pitfalls to avoid:

- Diverting the conversation to talk about yourself
- Talking too much out of a need to fill the silence
- Keeping silent when a response is indicated or failing to acknowledge what has been said
- Changing the subject, especially because of your own discomfort
- Offering false or cliché reassurance, such as "You'll do just fine!" It is inauthentic and inappropriate to promise what is impossible to predict.
- Making assumptions about what the person needs or wants

- Asking yes/no questions, which invite one-word answers
- Asking "Why?" questions, which can feel like an interrogation. Instead, ask concrete questions, such as "What motivated you to do that?"
- Belittling the person's feelings or equating their feelings with your own and other people's
- Giving advice or trying to fix the problem. If asked, "What should I do?" respond with "What do you want to do?" or "What do you see as your options right now?"
- Offering platitudes like "God helps those who help themselves" or "You made your bed, so now you have to lie in it." It is better to say something specific, clear, and relevant to the situation.
- Arguing. Respect their right to hold views different from yours.
- Interpreting the meaning of what you have been told: "That's because you left"; "That's because he's unreliable."
- Giving approval, disapproval, or value judgments
- Saying something that seems to wrap things up, stopping the flow of talk
- Complaining about how their problem is affecting you. If you need to talk about how you are being affected, talk to someone further removed from this person and their problem.[14]

---

[14] For more guidance on this, see Susan Silk and Barry Goldman, "How Not to Say the Wrong Thing," *Los Angeles Times*, April 7, 2013, articles.latimes.com/2013/apr/07/opinion/la-oe-0407-silk-ring-theory-20130407.

Of course, talking about oneself, especially about similar experiences, can sometimes be helpful to another person. Appendix C offers information on Emotional CPR, a training program that helps people develop empathic skills, and also some guidelines for when your conversation partner is exhibiting symptoms of a specific mental illness.

We do not always understand the importance and significance of listening to another person. In conversation it is often the case that while one person is talking, the other person is thinking of what they are going to say next, rather than listening closely to what the first is saying. In my training and experience both working as a spiritual director and being listened to by my own spiritual director, I know how precious simply listening is. It is a crucial part of being authentically present to the other.

THE DESIRE TO HELP, however well intended, can interfere with communication and be counterproductive. I am involved in a listening practice with an organization called Sidewalk Talk (www.sidewalk-talk.org). Sidewalk Talk listeners are trained in how to listen: giving full attention, practicing silence, being open to and curious about the other. The listener training for Sidewalk Talk is very clear that the desire to "fix" the person we are listening to breaks the human connection we have with them. It sets us up as an expert who knows better than they do how they should live their life and solve their problems. If someone asks for advice, it's better to respond with something like "What do you think your options are?" Often they have a very good idea what their options are and can, with encouragement, walk through the pros and cons of each one. If a solution comes from them, they are much more likely to enact it. On the other hand, if they accept a solution we offer, they are agreeing that we know better than they do, which harms their self-esteem, and if something goes awry, they may blame us.

Empathy

Sometimes when we don't know what to say but feel we have to say something, we resort to sympathy and minimization. Sympathy is feeling sorry for the person. However sincere, it is distancing, emphasizing the relative comfort and security of the person offering it as opposed to the pain and insecurity of the person receiving it. One can say, "I am sorry that this happened to you," and not "I feel sorry for you." And minimization, saying things like "It isn't so bad," "Cheer up," or "Pull yourself together," trivializes the person's pain. (When I was deeply depressed and suicidal, a friend told me that I just needed to drink more wine. This advice was not just useless but dangerous: People with depression should not consume depressants such as alcohol, and doing so can lead to them abusing alcohol in an effort to self-medicate and get relief from their condition.) Both sympathy and minimization may be well intentioned, but neither of them is helpful.

If someone is genuinely struggling with something, telling them that it isn't important or dismissing their difficulties doesn't help. Neither does offering sympathy, which means feeling pity for their misfortune. Rather, what helps is empathy. Empathy means seeing the world as the other sees it, being nonjudgmental, understanding the other's feelings, and communicating your understanding of those feelings.[15] Even though one can't completely know what another is feeling, empathy is the effort to adopt their point of view, to feel what they are feeling, and to let them know that you are conscious of their distress. It is allied with compassion, which means to "suffer with" the other person.

Hope

Even though being present, listening, and affirming can be enough, there are also helpful things you can say. Hope is the most powerful message that you can give a person who is struggling with mental illness and other mental health problems. Dr. Ragins has said that hope is the first stage in recovery from mental health problems.[16] All people need hope when they are struggling with something important. It's understandable to be concerned about making empty

---

[15] Theresa Wiseman, "A Concept Analysis of Empathy," *Journal of Advanced Nursing* 23, no. 6 (June 1996): 1162–67.

[16] David Clark, "'The Four Stages of Recovery,' from Mark Ragins," Recovery Stories, May 31, 2013, www.recoverystories.info/the-four-stages-of-recovery-from-mark-ragins.

promises, offering "false hope," but there are ways to give true hope.

I have personal experience of the importance of hope to people struggling with mental illness. I remember my first time in the psychiatric hospital, suffering from major depression and feeling utterly hopeless. When the doctor said he could help me, I only half believed him. When my family said they loved me, I didn't see how they could. But when a fellow patient told me how she had improved, I started to feel hope for myself. Her example showed me it was possible to get better. This is one of the reasons I believe peer support is so important.

People who are struggling with major or minor mental health problems need to be encouraged to continue working to build a meaningful life for themselves. This is especially true when they have had previous failures, maybe even harmful failures. Maybe there has been a suicide attempt or other kind of self-harm. Maybe they are ashamed of something they did in public and have lost faith that they can ever be accepted by society again. Maybe they have a criminal record for acts they committed when they were psychotic. Maybe they are worn down by long-lasting anxiety or depression. And recovery is often nonlinear, with progress intermixed with relapses; people may lose faith that they will ever be well, happy, or even functional.

Rather than expressing sympathy, you can respond empathetically by imagining what you would want to hear if you were in their position. You can offer words of encouragement and hope, a belief that things can get better, faith in the person and their strength. In *I Thought It Was Just Me (But It Isn't)*, empathy researcher Brené Brown explains that the more we practice empathy, the better we become at both giving and receiving it, and the more we understand how much courage and strength it takes for someone to be vulnerable enough to share their pain. We realize that our trials can make us stronger, that we can become strong in places where we were once fragile, and that sharing our pain with another person can help them heal.[17] This is a message of hope that you can give to someone who is brave enough to confide in you and let you in: that their strength in sharing with you is how you know that they are strong enough to get better.

Many people with mental illness suffer for years without a diagnosis or a treatment plan, and they may not fully understand their own needs. They just go along as best they can, making do with coping strategies that may be ineffective or even harmful. Being diagnosed with a mental illness may seem frightening, but for many it can open a door to better understanding and appropriate treatment. Affirming this can be a way of giving hope.

In my own theology, I find the holy to exist between people. A holy space is opened up when there is authentic communication, verbal or nonverbal, between someone whose

---

[17] Brené Brown, *I Thought It Was Just Me (But It Isn't): Making the Journey from "What Will People Think?" to "I Am Enough"* (New York: Avery, 2007).

mind is troubled and someone who is truly present with them, supporting them. And it is not only people who are seriously mentally ill who will be touched by this holiness, will respond to this authenticity. I think that most people will. But people who have suffered a blow to their self-image, such as that of a mental health crisis, have an especially sore need of it.

——————— DISCUSSION QUESTIONS ———————

1. Think about a truly difficult or terrible time in your life, and the things people said to you as you were going through it. Which felt good? Which felt bad?

2. Was there a time when someone was kind to you in a way that made a difference in your life?

3. How is human kindness expressed in your congregation, both formally and informally? Could more kindness be expressed, or could it be expressed in better ways? If so, how?

4. Has anyone's mere presence ever made a difference to you? Or have you ever seen someone's mere presence make a difference to someone else? If so, what were the circumstances?

5. Do you agree that holiness can exist between people? How does your personal theology deal with the power of presence?

6. Have you ever felt that someone was really listening to you? If so, what did it feel like? Have you ever wanted to be listened to but been treated dismissively instead? How did that feel?

7. What do you think of the guidelines for active listening and responding? Why do you think they say not to give advice? Would it be hard or easy for you to not give advice?

8. Can you think of a time when you felt hopeless? If so, what helped bring hope back into your life?

CREATING A SAFER PLACE

Where we had thought to be alone,
we should be with all the world.
—Joseph Campbell

A SAFE PLACE is one where a person can be honest and authentic about what they are going through, including mental health issues, without facing judgment, harassment, bias, or violence. Although no place can promise absolute safety from the negative attitudes of society, a congregation may be one of the safest places for a person with mental health challenges. In a faith community, they can be accepted and valued. And since every congregation will include many people affected by mental health problems, either their own or a loved one's, each person who is honest and authentic about their own struggles eases the collective pain of the congregation, even though they may never know it.

This chapter will focus on how individual laypeople can be helpful when people have mental health challenges.

Information specifically for leaders and ministers is included in appendix C.

Silence and secrecy are both the cause and the consequence of shame, prejudice, and discrimination, creating a vicious cycle that isolates people in their pain. Many people who find themselves facing a mental health problem, particularly for the first time, don't want to admit it to themselves, let alone their friends or neighbors. They may be afraid that someone will see them at their worst, when they may seem needy, unpredictable, incoherent, or incompetent. So they don't make their needs known to others—others who might bring meals, check in to see how they're doing, pray with them, offer encouragement and hope, and provide referrals.

And even when someone has been brave enough to speak about their mental illness, others tend to avoid talking about it and change the subject when it comes up. They may assume that the person doesn't want to talk about it: that they feel ashamed, that they want privacy. They may also worry about saying or doing the wrong thing, and even about their own safety if they get involved. So they don't ask the person how they're doing or what help they might want.

Because of the culture of silence around mental illness, you should not assume you know how many people in your congregation are affected by mental illness or who they are. Remember the story I told in the introduction: A family living with long-term mental illness, and now struggling with an acute crisis, was asked to provide support for another family coping with physical illness. And they accommodated this request, even though their own struggle was not being acknowledged and no one was supplying their needs.

In my mental health ministry, people often tell me about things that have made them feel it wasn't safe to be truthful about their own mental health challenges or those of a loved one. Even in Unitarian Universalist communities, people may say unkind words and make jokes about people with mental illness. Sometimes even a religious leader may do so. After all, we have all been shaped by culture and history, and for centuries mentally ill people have been mocked, feared, and tormented. People may use words like *crazy*, *nuts*, *loony*, or *insane* to describe negative behaviors or unpleasant situations. Or they may comment explicitly on mental illness in inaccurate and hurtful ways. For example, a woman whose daughter has a psychiatric disability and receives SSI benefits[18] reported that, in coffee hour after service, she has heard people say things like

- "People who are mentally ill look for the easy way out. Being too sympathetic is just rewarding bad behavior."
- "Most people with mental illness don't need medicine. I've had depression for years and I've never taken a pill."

---

[18] Supplemental Security Income (SSI) is a federal income supplement program for those who are aged or disabled and who have limited income and resources.

- "We spend too much money on handouts for able-bodied people who just don't feel like working. Putting those people to work could save the system for the elderly."
- "Of course that poor soul has mental illness; just look at their family."
- "Joan of Arc wasn't a saint or a visionary. She was psycho. Psycho and spiritual? Now that's a schizophrenic idea if I ever heard one."
- "Be careful of that man. He's been in and out of loony bins for years, and he never looks a person in the eye. He's probably dangerous."
- "My brother's out of the psych ward and now he's moved back in with my parents. He's never going to grow up or do something useful with his life unless they kick him out."

Most of these people did not know about her daughter's illness, and hearing them say these things made her feel her faith community wasn't a safe place for her to discuss it and get support for either herself or her daughter. I can fully understand why.

Since mental health problems are so prevalent, such negative comments hurt a lot of people. Often people with mental health problems internalize the negative stereotyping and come to have difficulty being fully themselves even to themselves. So it is especially important that such comments not be let slide. Congregation members should be encouraged to give support to people with mental health issues, and misconceptions and hurtful remarks should be gently pointed out. Everyone in the congregation can do this, serving as accountability partners for one another.

It is hard to say this, but it is true: Sometimes the people making negative remarks are people with mental health challenges themselves. They may be in denial, or they may be trying to act the way they think a person without a mental health challenge might act, hoping to convince themselves or others that they are not mentally troubled. After my first hospitalization, for depression, I did this myself. I didn't want anyone to know about my experience.

Supporting people with mental health problems and their families in our congregations means transforming the congregation so that things like this aren't said at coffee hour, or from the pulpit, or anywhere in congregational life. It also means offering acceptance. Rev. Mark Morrison-Reed shared with me an example of acceptance in his congregation:

> Nate was maybe in his thirties. He would sit in the front row rubbing his legs and rocking back and forth during the worship service. He was a bit awkward, his voice loud, and from time to time he would disappear.
>
> One weekday Donna [Mark's wife and co-minister] and I were at a bridge party with the senior members of the congregation. They were mostly in their eighties,

and we gathered in a nice suburban apartment. There were plenty of appetizers, serious card playing, and some light conversation until the hostess said, "I don't know how you put up with that young man fidgeting around throughout the service. It's just terrible."

What happened next left me stunned. One octogenarian said, "You do know it's his medication that makes him do that." A retired public health nurse told us she had spoken to him and knew what had been bothering him. A former university president said, "I was once institutionalized." And someone else said, "My son has bouts like that." Neither Donna nor I said a word.

My amazement turned to pride, and I knew why Nate kept coming to church. It was not about sermons, whether scholarly or entertaining. It was not about Universalism or our professed belief in a loving God. It was our lived theology, God made manifest in the love that surrounded that young man.

We need to live out the challenge of our faith. Love is the central question we are trying to answer with our lives. How do I love my neighbor, America, the world, myself? We know Universalism is about love, but so is Unitarianism, because it is about our Oneness—God's oneness and our own.

From the Pulpit

When I visit congregations as a community minister specializing in mental health issues, my usual practice is to use the sermon to tell some of my own story as a person living with mental health difficulties. I do this not because my own story is unusual but because I have learned that such self-disclosure from someone respected by congregation members can help make it safe for others to acknowledge mental illness of their own or in their families. At the end of the sermon I ask people to rise in body or spirit, as an act of "public witness," if they or a loved one is living with a mental health problem. Nearly every time I have done this, somewhere between three quarters and all of the congregation rises. Everyone looks around and can't believe so many people are affected. Afterward, coffee hour is abuzz with people telling formerly taboo stories. This is the single most effective way that I have discovered to begin dispelling the prejudice and discrimination that surround mental illness. Often, after such a sermon, people approach me in tears, thanking me for talking about this from the pulpit, saying that the service has given them hope. I believe that is why many people come to Sunday services: to get hope that will help them make it through the week. When a service like this is followed by congregational educational programs about mental health, especially when the program presenters include both mental health professionals and people who live with mental health challenges themselves, there are even greater increases in understanding and decreases in stigma.

It's important for people to talk about mental illness openly. It's important to talk about what it can feel like to come out as a person with a mental illness and experience love, affirmation, and acceptance. It's important to talk about how that experience heals internalized shame. Seeing someone do this publicly is incredibly powerful for those who are struggling to come to terms with their own mental health challenges. They can think, "Here is someone who understands, someone who won't judge, because they have been there."

It is not only ministers who can do this. In many congregations, laypeople have opportunities to preach, as well as to speak in other contexts. If you have had personal experience with mental health problems, you can tell your story in whatever context is available to you, and whether or not you have had such experiences, you can encourage others who have to tell their stories. Such an undertaking is an act of courage and a gift to the community, and it should be honored as such. But it is important to acknowledge that sometimes people aren't ready to tell such a personal story in a public setting; the first time I thought of telling my story in church, I became more and more nervous and finally had to back out of doing it a couple of weeks before the service was to happen. Several years later, I was able to tell my story without a problem. So encouragement to tell a story publicly is helpful, but being gracious when someone chooses not to is also helpful.

We can encourage our ministers and congregational leaders to routinely include mentions of mental illness in joys and concerns, sermons, prayers, and other parts of the worship service. For instance, a sermon that mentions groups of people who experience oppression could include the mentally ill, and requests for help for congregation members who are in difficulty could include (with permission) those facing mental health challenges.

A Mental Health Ministry

To become a safer place for people with mental health challenges, a congregation can create a mental health ministry that encompasses all members of the congregation and all aspects of congregational life. Laypeople can encourage congregational leaders to do this. To create such a ministry, a team should be formed whose members are committed to the issue; the team will work to involve the congregation as a whole in the ministry, as appropriate. Making this a congregation-wide project, rather than the purview of a small group, is key to changing the culture of the congregation so that it is helpful to people with mental health problems and their families.

The Unitarian Universalist Mental Health Network (uumentalhealth.org) offers a Caring Congregation Program (uumentalhealth.org/education/the-caring-congregation -curriculum) that includes nine steps for setting up a mental health ministry, first outlined by Gunnar Christiansen. Here is a modified version of these steps, which should be done in order:

1. Gain support from the minister and lay leadership. It is important that the people in power in the congregation agree that this work is important and should be carried out.

2. Make sure that your congregation has adequate guidelines for appropriate behavior: a covenant of right relations and a disruptive behavior policy. (These are discussed later in this chapter.)

3. Give worship services that focus on mental health.

4. Offer classes and educational programs on mental health. Rev. Susan Gregg-Schroeder's guide *Mental Illness and Families of Faith: How Congregations Can Respond* is one possibility. There are numerous other print and media resources on the Mental Health Ministries website (www.mentalhealthministries.net).

5. Ensure that the religious education program provides support for children with mental health problems themselves and for those whose parents or siblings have mental health problems. Congregations must commit to serving all children, weaving them into the fabric of the congregation. The best resource on this topic is Sally Patton's *Welcoming Children with Special Needs* (Boston: Unitarian Universalist Association, 2004).

6. Provide support groups for people with mental health problems and their families, or refer them to groups

elsewhere. Support groups can be located through local affiliates of the National Alliance on Mental Illness (NAMI) and other mental health organizations and through municipal, state, and community organizations.

7. Create a referral list of therapists, support groups, and community programs, and keep this list up-to-date. The easiest way to compile this list is to ask parishioners about therapists, psychiatrists, and other mental health professionals who have been helpful to them and whom they would be comfortable referring others to.

8. Encourage the congregation to establish a companioning program to care for people who may be struggling in worship services. (These programs are discussed later in this chapter.)

9. Advocate for providing pastoral care, spiritual support, and hospital visits for people with mental health problems who want such attention. This will require the pastoral care team to be educated about mental health; resources for this can be found in appendix C.

Challenges and Compassion

One of the biggest challenges that people with mental health problems face in participating in religious community is that they are often regarded as incapable, unable to know what's best for them, and having little to offer. As Unitarian

Universalists, we know that people with mental health problems, like all people, have inherent worth and dignity. It is important to give them agency and to listen to them about what they need.

As a Unitarian Universalist community minister, I have been contacted by many congregations that are facing a difficult situation involving a mental health problem and do not know how to respond or what to do. Ministers and other congregational leaders rarely have training to deal with serious mental illness; the topic is not taught in seminary, although some religious professionals may have had a chaplaincy experience in a mental health ward, and few lay leaders are also mental health professionals. They worry about how they can help the troubled person and their family while keeping the congregation safe for both them and others. They may fear that ministering to the person with a mental disorder could endanger the well-being of the rest of the congregation. But good outcomes are possible when the congregation's leadership and membership have the humility to recognize their lack of skills and refer people to appropriate professional resources while offering supportive community and unconditional love.

Many congregations worry about the presence of people with mental illness, sometimes going so far as to try to exclude them. But the truth of the matter is that they are already there, though they may be hiding. And the more hostility they sense, the more they will hide, and perhaps even express such hostility themselves in an effort to disguise themselves and fit in. Religious and lay leaders, and all members of the congregation, should understand that mental health problems are so common that there is no way to exclude people affected by them.

It is certainly important to keep the congregation safe from behavior that could be disruptive to its functioning or even dangerous. A behavior is disruptive if it interferes with the running of the congregation's programs or if it is intentionally mean, bullying, or aggressive toward leaders or others in the congregation. If someone is seriously disrupting congregational activity, it isn't doing them or the community any favors to let them continue, whether or not they have a diagnosed mental disorder. Depending on the congregation's disruptive behavior policy, they may need to be gently or firmly told that this behavior can't continue, and they may need to take a break from participating in congregational life for a while.

However, it is important not to assume that because a person has a mental illness, they will have problematic behavior. I have heard stories of people being exiled from their congregations because they confided to a church leader that they had a mental illness and were having problems finding therapy or adequate medication. This really saddens me. I have been working with people with mental health problems for many years, and I know how hard it is sometimes to find an effective combination of medicines. It can be a lengthy process of trial and error, experimenting with different medications and combinations of medications, at varying doses, and staying on each new trial for months before its success or failure is clear. Some people have to settle for a medication regimen that isn't completely effective and that may have significant side effects, such as rapid weight gain or some other serious problem. Some give up on medication and look for alternative ways to get relief, which might involve substance abuse. Sometimes they can't access mental health care, because they aren't adequately insured or because they hold marginalized identities that are discriminated against by the medical community. And sometimes, despite treatment, they relapse after a few months.

I am troubled by the suggestion that people in such situations should in effect be exiled from the congregation, when acceptance by loving, open-minded people could have helped them integrate into it. Such rejection can be discouraging, and people can start to lose hope when it is just at this time that they most need a supportive community. I believe that forcing them to choose between staying in the congregation and keeping their mental health situation a secret, or being banished until they can find the right medication and stay on it without a relapse, can adversely affect their mental health. It certainly doesn't help it.

When evaluating someone's disruptive behavior, it is also crucial to consider whether the person is in fact calling out oppression in the congregation. If so, the situation should be acknowledged and leaders should take action to correct it.

An issue that often comes up when discussing mental illness is the fear that a mentally ill person might be violent. In television shows, movies, and books, a common trope involves such a person going berserk and attacking someone. Unfortunately, this results in a widespread fear of people who live with mental illness among the population at large. The reality is that people who live with mental illness are much more likely to be victims rather than perpetrators of violence. The only exception is that an actively psychotic person who is also abusing alcohol or drugs is slightly more likely to become violent than is the average person. People struggling with both a substance abuse problem and a mental health problem need specialized support. Resources for situations where people have both an addiction and a mental illness are addressed in appendix C.

Many people with significant and pervasive maladaptive behaviors were abused in childhood and developed these behaviors as a way of coping with the abuse. Research has shown that experiencing a traumatic event such as abuse, neglect, parental substance abuse, parental divorce, parental incarceration, or domestic violence before the age of eighteen increases the likelihood of a variety of negative outcomes in adulthood, including poor physical and mental health, substance abuse, and other problematic behavior.[19]

---

[19] "Adverse Childhood Experiences (ACEs)," Child Welfare Information Gateway, a service of the Children's Bureau, Administration for Children and Families, United States Department of Health and Human Services, www.childwelfare.gov/topics/preventing/preventionmonth/resources/ace.

People with this kind of trauma history can present challenging behavior in congregational settings. They might show excessive fear of abandonment and cling to others, or they might have outbursts of inappropriate anger. Understanding the reasons for their behavior might help fellow congregation members find good ways to intervene, especially if the person recognizes there is a problem and is making a good-faith effort to change. Others can help by encouraging them to seek effective therapy and keep working to ameliorate their behavior, by giving them positive feedback when they do, and by enforcing kind but firm boundaries when problematic behavior recurs.

People who have experienced or are experiencing mental health struggles bring their congregations real gifts: the compassion, spiritual wisdom, and practice of unconditional acceptance they may have learned the hard way, and a chance for the congregation to live out its values. Also, all congregants can see how people with mental illness are treated, and will know that they will likely be treated the same way when they themselves are in crisis and need love and support. The practices and skills that make a congregation a

---

For overviews of this research, see Julia Herzog and Christian Schmahl, "Adverse Childhood Experiences and the Consequences on Neurobiological, Psychosocial, and Somatic Conditions across the Lifespan," *Frontiers in Psychiatry* 9 (2018): 420; Vincent J. Felitti et al., "Relationship of Childhood Abuse and Household Dysfunction to Many of the Leading Causes of Death in Adults: The Adverse Childhood Experiences (ACE) Study," *American Journal of Preventive Medicine* 14, no. 4 (May 1998): 245–58, doi.org/10.1016/S0749-3797(98)00017-8.

safe place for people living with a mental illness make it a better, safer, more spiritually enriching, and more loving place for everyone. Encouraging and advocating for education on mental health in the congregation can be helpful to all its members, professionals and laypeople alike.

There are certain rare situations that a congregation must admit, in all humility, that it cannot safely handle. Rev. Mark Belletini told me of one:

> In one larger congregation, a new member brought boisterousness and clear intelligence, and at first, people drew closer to him. But as the months passed, it was clear that something else was happening.
>
> He was threatening people who disagreed with him with violence, literally fisticuffs. He came into the office of the lead minister and insisted he fire the director of lifespan education—"just because," he said, "I don't like her." The minister told him that was entirely inappropriate and asked him to leave the office. After this, the minister consulted a psychiatrist in the congregation, and she suggested that his behavior seemed to be due to an untreated narcissistic disorder, and that his threats, which were continuing, needed to be taken seriously. The minister also heard that several members of the board had approached the man to remind him of the congregation's covenant of respectful relations, which had been made clear to him before he signed the membership book

and which he was now violating. He responded, "That doesn't apply to me" and dismissed the board members.

The minister brought all of this evidence up to the board, which immediately agreed that his membership needed to be rescinded because he had fallen out of covenant and that it was important to do this in order to keep the congregation safe.

Sometimes members believe that because we have "Universalism" in our name, we should let a disruptive person devastate a congregation. And considering asking someone to leave a congregation is very difficult for everyone involved, both those in leadership and members who may have had a relationship with the person. But even Universalists have to have boundaries and limits. And a congregation's board needs to understand this and take whatever action is warranted.

If someone's behavior is destructive and they can't or won't modify it, there is no easy way out: The person needs to go. But if they are struggling and seeking help, then acceptance, empathy, and compassion will be the kindest response in both the short run and the long run. In both cases the decision whether or not to expel someone is taken by the congregation's leadership. Congregation members can assist by helping leaders understand what is happening and why, and by standing up for someone who may be vulnerable and need an advocate. They may need to be careful not to violate confidentiality and not to get inappropriately involved. Talking the situation over with a minister or spiritual director can help.

Covenant of Right Relations and Disruptive Behavior Policy

Explaining to someone that their behavior is not acceptable can be difficult, and the conversation can have ripple effects throughout the congregation. It helps to have clear policies about what constitutes unacceptable behavior and how it should be responded to. All congregations should have a covenant of right relations and a disruptive behavior policy; these are important parts of addressing mental health difficulties in congregations, and are useful in other contexts as well. The UUA's *Becoming a Safer Congregation: A Guide to Effective Safety Policies and Practices* (www.uua.org/safe/handbook) discusses the importance of these policies and how to establish them.

All members of the congregation, whether in leadership roles or not, should be familiar with the congregation's covenant of right relations and disruptive behavior policy. Those concerned with offering support and welcome to people with mental health problems should help develop them. When grappling with mental illness in a congregational setting, it is key to remember that the covenant is a statement of mutuality, forgiveness, and renewal, and that it includes all people in the congregation. We must treat each person, no matter what their mental health status, in accordance with our seven Principles, beginning by respecting their inherent worth and dignity. Of course, respecting their inherent worth and dignity does not mean passively accepting their destructive behavior. If someone is unwilling or unable to abide by the covenant, we need to tell them that as long as that is the case, they unfortunately cannot remain in the congregation.

Sometimes religious or spiritual people accept things that they should not. As hard as it may be, it is important to set and enforce boundaries on acceptable behavior in a congregation. A disruptive behavior policy should define what constitutes unacceptable behavior and specify what will be done if it occurs. If someone is to be asked to leave the congregation for a time, the policy should set out the circumstances under which they can return.

Some congregations' disruptive behavior policies may include the option of calling the police in certain situations. The Unitarian Universalist Association does not recommend this.[20] American police forces are ill-equipped to handle mental health crises and have an ongoing pattern of racialized violence. It has happened far too often that police officers called to restrain or remove a person having a mental health crisis have killed them. The son of a friend of mine was killed this way.

[20] Unitarian Universalist Association, "Stop Calling the Police and Start Eradicating Anti-Blackness," June 2, 2020, https://www.uua.org/pressroom/press-releases/stop-calling-police-start-eradicating-anti-blackness

If police must be called, whenever possible they should be asked to send officers trained in crisis intervention through CIT International (www.citinternational.org). CIT programs are used by many police departments, and the techniques they teach are very effective in de-escalating mental health crises. However, congregations should consider the possible ramifications of involving the police before a crisis arises. Research social workers, mediation hotlines, and other first responders in your area to have alternative sources of backup on hand.

Examples of covenants and disruptive behavior policies can be found in "The Care of Difficult People" (uumental health.org/education/handouts-from-workshops/), a handout I gave in a workshop on handling disruptive behavior. The UUA's Safe Congregations website (www.uua.org/safe) also offers a great deal of information and guidance. Remember that these covenants and policies apply to everyone in the congregation, not just people with mental illness.

Companioning Programs

What if a person with a mental illness is disruptive during a worship service, small group session, social event, or other programming? The best way that I have seen to handle such situations is to develop a companioning program. Rev. Dr. Craig Rennebohm has beautifully described the companionship ministry he carried out with homeless people in the

Seattle area for more than two decades.[21] In a congregational setting, people are trained to be "companions" who are on the lookout for problems during the worship service. If they see someone having difficulties, whether they know the person or not, they sit next to them and talk to them quietly and calmly. If the person is still being disruptive, they calmly offer to accompany the person out of the sanctuary and sit with them outside, giving them attention, listening to them, hearing their story. This is not *getting rid* of someone; it is *taking care* of them. It is living out a theology of love. And it makes a tremendous difference in a congregation.

Companionship can be a one-time or occasional support offered on the spot in a service. Or it can be part of an ongoing relationship with someone who wants to be a member of the congregation and is experiencing difficulties. In the former case, the person doesn't formally consent to having a companion; someone just steps forward to offer companionship. In the latter, the person consents to a continuing mutual relationship. In both cases, companionship includes these basic spiritual practices:

- providing hospitality by approaching a person with respect, honoring their inherent dignity,

---

[21] Craig Rennebohm with David Paul, *Souls in the Hands of a Tender God: Stories of the Search for Home and Healing on the Streets* (Boston: Beacon Press, 2008).

- discovering what we have in common, setting aside our power and privilege and meeting as equals, acknowledging our common humanity,
- learning to share a person's journey side by side, without pressuring them or imposing our own priorities,
- learning how to listen, realizing that a listening presence is a gift, and learning how to respond, and
- hearing what the person tells us about what they need and supporting them by connecting them with community resources to help build a circle of care.

Companioning programs are usually started by a minister, congregational leader, or committee in a congregation that focuses on mental health issues. Congregation members can advocate for such a program and consider training to be companions. More information and resources are available from the Companionship Movement (www .thecompanionshipmovement.org).

───────── DISCUSSION QUESTIONS ─────────

1. Have you ever heard a worship service focused on mental health? If so, what was it like? If not, why do you think your congregation hasn't held one?

2. Why do you think so many people speak up when asked to offer a public witness about mental health? Why do you think they are surprised at the numbers of others who do so as well? Would you answer such a call for public witness? Why or why not?

3. A service about mental health issues may help some people realize how prevalent such issues are. Do you think this realization will last or be forgotten?

4. What do you think you as a congregation member can do when other members make inappropriate comments about mental illness? If your congregation has a covenant of right relations, would such comments violate it?

5. Does your congregation have a disruptive behavior policy and/or a covenant of right relations? If not, would you advocate for creating one?

6. Why do you think some congregations put stringent limits on the membership of people with mental illness? Do you think such limits are a good idea?

7. What do you think of the idea of a companioning ministry? Would you want your congregation to establish such a ministry? Is there anyone in your congregation who would make a good companion? Would you consider being one yourself?

8. Has your congregation been challenged by the behavior of someone who had a mental health problem? What were the circumstances? What was done? Would you do the same thing again?

FACING THE ULTIMATE CRISIS: SUICIDE

Suicide prevention is everyone's business.
—American Association for Suicidology

IN DEALING WITH people who have mental illness, many people worry about the risk of suicide. It is frightening to think that someone might end their life. Could you help prevent a suicide? What if you do the wrong thing? Many congregations have had members die by suicide. Whether or not there was any warning, such a death is deeply troubling to many parishioners, especially those who were close to the person who died.

Suicidal ideation (thinking about suicide) is more common than is usually understood. Many people in difficulty have thought, at least briefly, that their best option is to take their own life. But most don't make an attempt. Still, professional mental health counseling plays a key role in responding to suicidal ideation. Professionals can hospital-ize and treat a person who is actively suicidal, protecting them until they can safely be released. The lives of most people treated this way are saved.

Congregations can only do so much to help someone who is seriously intent on taking their life, but they can play a role, alongside the mental health professionals. They do this by practicing the elements that have been discussed in this book. Still, it is important to remember that, while con-gregation members can offer invaluable support, they are not responsible for what happens. They must not assume that if they do everything right, they'll always be able to "save" someone. They may offer understanding and sup-port, and the person may die by suicide anyway. This is not their fault. Even the best of intentions, thorough preparation, and ideal supportive actions—the best practices possible—are not always sufficient. Also, sometimes suicides happen impulsively.

Rev. Mark Belletini told me about a minister who spoke with a suicidal colleague and friend every day for a month and a half. When the winter holidays began, however, they were both so engaged with congregational events that they stopped the daily phone calls. After the New Year, the friend said that he was not in such a despondent state anymore and wanted to live. Educated and self-aware, he knew he was sus-ceptible to having depression, but he insisted it had abated. They still spoke in January, but less often, and mostly about professional things; they also laughed together a lot. And then in mid-February, the friend took his own life. The minister fell into despair himself, wondering whether there was anything else he could have said or done to save his friend's life. Ultimately he decided he needed support and sought out a therapist, who helped him understand and cope with his shock, grief, and anger.

Surviving a dear friend's suicide and moving on is some of the hardest work we can ever do. And surviving a member's suicide and moving on is some of the hardest work a congregation can ever do.

Authenticity

I once took a class called "Disarming the Suicidal Mind."[22] The instructor, Dr. Timothy Spruill, worked with a hospital emergency department in his hometown in Florida. He was called into the hospital whenever a person came into the emergency room after a suicide attempt. His job was to talk to them and try to understand the situation, judge the risk that they would try again, and begin the process of getting them help. He had worked with thousands of such people, and his class covered a wide range of information: statistics and trends, suicide rates by age and gender, factors that make suicide attempts more likely, how to assess the risk that

---

[22] Recordings of this program in a variety of formats, as well as in-person classes, are available from PESI (www.pesi.com).

someone will make an attempt, and more. He also discussed approaches and therapies that are used to get people through the experience and on to a more hopeful way of thinking.

The people at greatest risk of suicide tend to believe they are a burden to their loved ones. They are likely to feel isolated and to think that their situation is hopeless. And they may have practiced overcoming their fear of death, including by previous suicide attempts. We asked Dr. Spruill what he had found to be most helpful in talking to his patients, and he said, "Find something you can like about the person, and concentrate on that when you talk to them." Most, he said, can tell immediately when someone is talking down to them, or treating them like a laboratory specimen or a worthless human being. They probably already think of themselves as worthless, and treating them that way only confirms that belief. Authenticity is the key element here. Authentically connecting with someone and recognizing their worth require genuinely liking something about them. Consciously or subconsciously, they can sense that liking, and it tells them that perhaps they aren't worthless after all. Dr. Spruill found this to be true no matter what therapeutic or psychiatric technique was being used.

In a congregational setting, behaving with authenticity means finding something you can honestly and genuinely like about a congregation member who is struggling emotionally and concentrating on that while interacting with them. This is important, for example, when someone shares, in a small group or during Joys and Concerns, that they are having emotional difficulties; when a member of a congregational mental health group seems to be especially troubled; or when someone tearfully acknowledges that they are considering suicide. Really, it's important whenever we meet someone, because we never know what they are struggling with.

Hope, Empathy, and Compassion

People who are suicidal have lost hope. They are in such psychological pain, feel so strongly that they are a burden to others, and are so unable to see an end to their suffering that the only solution they can think of is to make an end to their life. Many survivors of suicide attempts report that they didn't really want to die; they just wanted to stop hurting and couldn't see another way.

I have volunteered for an organization called Bridgewatch Angels (www.facebook.com/www.bridgewatchangels .org). Knowing that there is often a suicide cluster on holidays, the Bridgewatch Angels dedicate their holidays to saving lives on the Golden Gate Bridge. Every Christmas, Thanksgiving, New Year's, Valentine's Day, and Memorial Day, they recruit and train two shifts of volunteers to be present on the bridge. The volunteers greet everyone they meet with smiles and good wishes, but they go further by engaging with anyone on the bridge who is walking alone, displaying negative, slumping body posture, or lingering mid-span. They offer support to these people by listening and sharing words of life and hope, and in doing so they have saved many lives.

Bridgewatch volunteers certainly call for professional mental health workers when they encounter someone who is suicidal, but they are also trained in what to say to the person while waiting for professional help to arrive. Members of a congregation should also know this, because they might someday find themselves in a conversation with another member who says they are contemplating suicide. This might happen in a small group ministry setting where sharing is encouraged, or between close friends, or even with a near stranger in coffee hour. Here are Bridgewatch's suggestions of things to say:

- "You are not alone. I'm here to listen. I care about you."
- "What kinds of thoughts are you having? Can you tell me more about that?"
- "There is nothing more important than your life."
- "You may not believe it now, but the way you're feeling will change." (This is appropriate if the person's suicidality is impulsive, triggered by a painful experience such as a break-up or a fight with parents.)
- "I may not be able to understand exactly how you feel, but I care about you and want to help."
- "Could you hold off one more day, hour, or minute . . . whatever you can manage? There is help available."

- "This must be so hard for you. I can tell how real your pain is."
- "There are people who love you and want to support you, even though it doesn't feel like that right now."
- "There are help and resources available to support you."
- Or you could say nothing at all and just listen, listen, listen.

All of these responses offer hope to the suicidal individual.

As a contrast, here are things *not* to say to a suicidal person. These comments intensify blame, reinforce a belief that no one will help them, and increase hopelessness and despair:

- "Suicide is selfish."
- "There are people who have it worse than you."
- "I get sad sometimes too."
- "Suicide is the easy way out."
- "Are you doing this for attention?"
- "Think how your family will feel."
- "I don't want to talk about this."
- "You're not praying enough."
- "Have you taken your meds?"
- "You need to relax."
- "I would be suicidal too in your position."

Referrals, Reporting, and Confidentiality

Whenever someone says that they are contemplating suicide, professional mental health care should be consulted. It is better to be safe than sorry. The QPR Institute (qprinstitute.com) suggests three simple steps:

Q: Question a person about whether they are suicidal.

P: Persuade them to get help.

R: Refer them to an appropriate resource.

Ask the person if they are getting professional care and if so, whether they've discussed their suicidal ideation with their caregiver. If they are not already working with a professional, they need a referral. Sometimes someone who is suicidal may refuse to accept help or a referral. Even if they have told you about their thoughts in confidence, you may need to break confidentiality if you believe that their life is in danger. In the near term, the person may be angry with you for doing so, but it's worth it to save their life. Calling 911 is one way to get immediate help. If the situation is not an emergency, you can inform the minister. In some states, ministers are mandated reporters in situations where there is a threat of harm to self or others, so informing the minister will result in action being taken.

After Suicide

If there has been a suicide in the congregation, people often don't know what to say to the person's family. But saying nothing, ignoring the subject and the family, can be painful for them and perpetuate the stigma around suicide. Here are some helpful things that you can say:

- "I am so sorry for your loss."
- "I know how much you love [use the person's name]. This must be very difficult for you."
- "I am willing to talk with you about this. Or, if you don't want to talk right now, that is okay, too."
- "Can I, or the congregation, do something for you? A meal, an errand, . . . ?"
- "I don't know what to say, but I am here for you."

You might also share good memories of the person. Be patient with grieving family members, and remain present with them.

Here are some things that are not helpful to say:

- "Oh, no! What happened?"
- "I know exactly how you feel."
- "They're in a better place now."

It is also never helpful to assign blame for the death.

In the aftermath of a suicide, congregation members can help those who are grieving by practicing the elements discussed in this book: acceptance, presence, authenticity, hope, compassion, empathy, listening, and taking care. Professional mental health care may also be required. There are support groups that specialize in working with families where there has been a suicide, and it can be helpful to have a list of such local groups available, so that the minister or pastoral care team can make referrals. A layperson could advocate for the creation of such a list or create it themselves.[23]

---

[23] The American Association of Suicidology provides one list at suicidology .org/resources/support-groups.

—————— DISCUSSION QUESTIONS ——————

1. Has someone in your congregation or someone you knew well ever died by suicide? What kinds of feelings did this bring up in you or in members of your congregation?

2. If you are comfortable sharing this, have you ever had suicidal thoughts yourself? If you have, what helped you?

3. Why do you think that people who are considering suicide are helped when they believe someone truly likes them?

4. Would you be comfortable urging a suicidal person to accept professional help? If not, why? If so, how would you do this?

5. What do you think of the Bridgewatch Angels' suggestions for what to say and not to say to suicidal people?

TAKING CARE OF PEOPLE

Caring is the greatest thing.
Caring matters most.
  —Last words of Frederich Von Hugel

SOME PEOPLE HAVE brief, situational mental health problems that they get over and that don't recur. For other people, such problems can be long term: perhaps chronic, or perhaps recurring with varying levels of intensity. It has been more than forty years since I was hospitalized with my first serious bout of depression. I have had ups and downs since then, at times just barely coping day to day and at other times doing fairly well. I can say that, in general, I am much better off mentally now than I have been at some times in the past. But sometimes life throws me a curveball, and I once again feel depressed. Over the years, I've learned what triggers a problem and what works to pull me out of the depths. These lessons are very important.

Below are some suggestions of ways that both people living with mental health challenges and people who care for them can cope with those challenges. They are not professional medical advice, just things that have worked for real people I have spoken with. Of course, not every suggestion will work for every person. Each person and family would do well to create their own list of options and tools. If someone in your congregation is struggling, you can encourage them to consider the suggestions here or use the list to research alternatives for them.

Many people have difficulty accessing mental health care because of financial, cultural, geographic, and personal factors. People usually begin looking for a therapist or psychiatrist by getting a list of approved providers from their insurance company or asking their friends for recommendations. It can be difficult to find a practitioner who is taking new patients or who can see someone quickly when the situation is urgent. Moreover, some people may need to see a practitioner with a particular skill or specialty: someone who speaks a specific language, for instance, or someone who works with teens, or transgender people, or people of color.

Even for those who have insurance, the cost of care can be a challenge. Many psychiatrists and therapists don't take insurance, so patients must pay out of pocket. Alternative therapies are often not covered by insurance, so they too are out-of-pocket expenses. And even when care is covered, many insurance companies limit the number of visits for which they will pay.

All these factors can make it difficult for people to get adequate therapy for their mental health problems. However, there are options and resources other than paying to see a traditional doctor or mental health professional. Peer and self-help groups sometimes offer very fine free programs; others may be available through local government organizations or universities. Support is also available online, both self-guided and in groups. Some research will help determine what is available in your community and what is and isn't covered by insurance. Additionally, many of the suggestions here cost nothing; they are a matter of making a lifestyle change.

Things the Person with Mental Health Difficulties Can Do

Get Professional or Peer Help

- Enter psychotherapy with a therapist whose skills match your particular needs.
- Work with a psychiatrist to find effective medication in an effective dosage, and take it as prescribed.
- Join a peer support group.
- Consider adding alternative therapies to your treatment plan. Among the possibilities are acupuncture, acupressure, homeopathic treatments, dance therapy, art therapy, music therapy, tai chi, and yoga.

- Help someone else, especially someone with problems similar to yours.
- Work with a counselor to identify your career goals, and work toward them.

Care for Your Body

- Eat a balanced diet.
- Consume little or no caffeine. It can make some people anxious and jumpy.
- Avoid alcohol. It is a depressant and often interferes with medication.
- Get plenty of rest. If you can't sleep, ask your doctor for something to help you.

Manage Your Stress

- Exercise. Unless your doctor cautions against it, do something—walking, jogging, aerobics, swimming, sports—to elevate your heart rate for fifteen to thirty minutes a day.
- Don't commit yourself to too many activities, which can make you feel overwhelmed.

Be Aware of Your Emotions

- Learn how to recognize signs that an episode of mental illness may be imminent.
- When those signs appear, take immediate action to head the episode off or minimize it. One possibility is to get to a safe place and do something that lets you

laugh, cry, or get angry. Involve your family, so they can help you.

- Develop a Wellness Recovery Action Plan (WRAP; mentalhealthrecovery.com). WRAP is a self-designed, evidence-based prevention and wellness process that anyone can use. I have seen it make a difference in the lives of people with serious mental illness, and I recommend it highly. WRAP guides you to
  - discover your own simple, safe wellness tools, such as journaling and peer counseling,
  - develop a daily routine that promotes your mental health,
  - identify early warning signs that things are getting worse,
  - create an action plan for how to respond at these times,
  - create a crisis plan that will identify when others need to take over responsibility for your care, and what is and is not helpful to you at such a time, and
  - create a post-crisis plan, laying out what to do after you have come out of the crisis.

Enrich Your Life

- Do some creative activity, such as music, drawing, painting, crafts, creative writing, or weaving.
- Take an adult education class. For instance, you could explore an academic topic such as history, or practice a creative art, or learn a sport.

- Do volunteer work.
- Do things with friends, and try to develop new friendships.
- Seek out helpful relatives.

Engage with Your Spirituality

- Consider the fact that there is no one else on Earth quite like you. Think of your valuable personal qualities and creative abilities, and appreciate them. This helps you to come to love yourself.
- Meditate. Try to spend fifteen minutes to an hour on a regular basis quietly listening to your heartbeat and breathing, or find a guided meditation program. Be aware, however, that meditation can be disturbing for some people who are actively psychotic. If you are dealing with psychosis, and meditation is disturbing, then stop meditating.

Mental health problems are challenges not only for the people who are ill but also for those who are supporting and caring for them: most often their family members, sometimes their close friends. Care must be consistent, which means that caregivers must be persistent. The need to stay with the person through both the plateaus in their progress and the regressions or flare-ups, making sure they know they are always loved unconditionally, can be exhausting and spiritually draining, and the difficulty is often compounded by guilt and self-blame. Even during the "good times," family members and friends know that things can change dramatically with almost no warning; they are walking on eggshells. The congregation can play a major role in caring for the caretakers.

Caring for caretakers is often much less threatening or intimidating to a congregant than working directly with the person with a mental health problem, and it requires much less training and preparation. An important part of that training is learning how to create safer places for both people with mental health challenges and those caring directly for them (see chapter 4). The first workshop in the Caring Congregation Curriculum (see appendix C) is one source of this training.

The following is a list of strategies I have collected from family members of people with mental health problems, suggesting ways they can help both their family member and themselves. A congregant who wants to help a caregiver might do or suggest any of these.

Things Family Members Can Do

Get Professional or Peer Help

- A therapist can help you discern what your responsibilities and capabilities are.
- Emergency responders can provide immediate attention for someone in danger. If someone is actively suicidal, call 911.

- Join a support group, whether formal or informal, for families of those living with mental illness. Start one at your congregation if you cannot find one.
- If necessary, arrange for someone to stay with the mentally ill person while you are at the group; this is a good opportunity for your congregation to offer support.
- If the mentally ill person also has a co-occurring addiction, attend Al-Anon or Nar-Anon meetings, as appropriate. If local groups are too Christian or Evangelically oriented to be helpful to you, investigate AA Agnostica (aaagnostica.org), AA beyond Belief (aabeyondbelief .org), or Secular AA (secularaa.org) for online support or help starting a local group. See "Addiction-Specific Resources" in appendix C for more information on co-occurring addictions.
- Learn all you can about the mental health problem affecting the individual.
- Attend classes given by local mental health advocacy groups and treatment centers. Some, including excellent ones from the National Alliance on Mental Illness (nami.org), are available online.

Communicate Effectively

- Tell the person that you care about them no matter how difficult the situation is.
- If they are open to having visitors, visit them, especially if they are hospitalized. A smile, a flower, a picture, or a short hug can make all the difference.

- Avoid doing things that trigger the person's disorder. For instance, if they become anxious or depressed when they are pressured to hurry, don't try to rush things.
- Be flexible and patient. Cures are almost never instantaneous.

Help the Person Live with the Illness

- Help the person keep their days structured.
- Support their efforts to find the medicines and therapies that work best.
- Monitor their medicine intake. This is often an area of conflict between the person and their family, so proceed carefully. Try to position yourself as an ally of both your family member and their doctor.
- Encourage them to exercise, eat a good diet, get plenty of sleep, pursue creative activities, and get out in the sunlight. Offer to join the person in their activities. This will help with your own physical and mental health as well. Some people with mental health problems find themselves staying awake in the night and sleeping during the day, which can disrupt the structure you are trying to help them maintain. Making appointments to meet for breakfast or an early walk can help establish a routine.
- Learn to recognize the warning signs that an episode is imminent and how to help your loved one head it off or minimize it. One of the best ways to do this is by taking a Mental Health First Aid course (see appendix

C). If one is not offered locally, consider sponsoring this course at your congregation.

- Work with the person on their Wellness Recovery Action Plan (WRAP; see appendix C), and consider playing whatever role in it you can.
- Maintain some kind of regular social activity with your loved one, such as going to the movies.
- Plan activities for both of you to look forward to.
- Make the best of their good days. Drop routine or low-priority tasks like housework to enjoy time with them.
- Keep guns out of the house. Having this kind of lethal weapon easily available makes suicide more likely.

Have a Life of Your Own

- If the person you are caring for needs monitoring or assistance, get help. If you cannot afford to hire help, work with your minister or your congregation's pastoral care team to fill this need.
- Plan fun and restorative activities for yourself alone.
- Live one day at a time.

──────── DISCUSSION QUESTIONS ────────

1. Mental health issues can be chronic, and dealing with them can be a long-term concern. Would it be difficult for your congregation to work with a person and a family over the long term? If so, what might make it easier? Are there local resources that might help?

2. What do you think about how difficult it can be for people, especially those with limited economic means, people of color, and LGBTQ people, to get adequate mental health care? Many people say that the mental health system is broken. Do you agree?

3. Which of the suggested lifestyle changes would you find easy to make? Which would you find difficult?

4. Do you think that your spirituality or theology helps you to stick with something difficult for the long haul?

BEYOND THE WALLS

All advocacy is, at its core,
an exercise in empathy.
—Samantha Power

EVERY THURSDAY AFTERNOON, a spiritual director colleague and I set up chairs on the sidewalk in the Tenderloin
district of San Francisco, one of the city's poorest neighbor-
hoods. We are there to listen to people. We listen to whatever they want to talk about, without giving advice or judging
them. Our presence there is a project of the Faithful Fools
Street Ministry (faithfulfools.org), which works to shatter
myths about those living in poverty and to see their light,
courage, intelligence, strength, and creativity. This ministry
participates in Sidewalk Talk (www.sidewalk-talk.org), which
offers such listening in communities across the country,
with the goal of destigmatizing mental illness.

The Tenderloin district is quite poor. Most of the people
we meet on the street are Black, with some Latinos and

Asian Americans and only a few European Americans. If they have half of their teeth, they are lucky. Drug and mental health problems are common. A lot of people are on the street at all hours, sitting, talking, or walking around.

When my colleague and I began our ministry, residents of the Tenderloin were wary of us, wondering why we were there. But before long, people started to share some in-depth stories of their lives. When I explained to one man that we weren't selling anything or trying to convert anyone, he asked, "Then why do you come? What's in it for you?" I said, "I have the satisfaction of knowing I am helping to make the world a friendlier place." He said, "OK, then, I'll talk to you." He was from Ethiopia and had lived in Russia, Germany, and finally the United States. He spoke five languages and had had many jobs and adventures. He landed in this poor neighborhood because he developed a mental illness and is on disability.

Another man wanted to talk to me about a near-death experience he had when he was a boy. None of his friends or relatives had ever wanted to hear about it, and he was grateful that I would listen. He had a very active spiritual life and felt that he was in the presence of angels. He asked about me and was surprised when I told him I was a minister. He told me that I might meet him in heaven some day and we would talk about how we had met on the sidewalk in San Francisco and had a conversation. Though I don't share his theology, the image was very moving to me. What more could I have been doing with my life that day than to be there to listen to that man?

Our society has not fully come to grips with how to treat people who have mental illness. They may be ostracized, hospitalized, jailed, forcibly medicated, or ignored. Psychiatrists and therapists are often not available to them, either because they cannot afford the fees (even if they have insurance) or because free or low-cost professionals are carrying overwhelming caseloads already. The mental health system is a broken one in which the people with the most serious illnesses receive the least care. And if a mentally ill person is marginalized in some additional way—if they are elderly, of color, disabled, or LGBTQ, for instance—their situation is likely to be even worse.

People with limited resources, which includes many people of color, must rely only on the public mental health system, in which the options are often very limited. Although psychiatric hospitals may be available in acute situations, it is common for the public system to provide only medication and one brief (fifteen- to twenty-minute) visit with a psychiatrist every three or four months, with no psychotherapy or alternative therapy at all. Further, the public mental health system doesn't always validate the spiritual dimension of mental health.

LGBTQ people may find it difficult to find a therapist or doctor who will be understanding and supportive, and may fear even trying to do so; after all, the American Psychiatric

Association considered homosexuality a mental illness until 1973. It may be especially difficult for transgender people to find adequate psychotherapy, as understanding of trans issues and identities lags even among medical practitioners. If you are an LGBTQ person seeking care, looking for therapists who specialize in LGBTQ issues can help bridge this gap.

Finding competent care can be similarly difficult for people of color. There are striking disparities between white people and people of other racial and ethnic backgrounds in access to culturally responsive mental health services and in the quality of services they do receive.[24] The American medical system's history of racial bias and unequal treatment means that these communities are often mistrustful of such institutions, especially as mental health care itself has been used to discriminate against doubly marginalized populations such as Black and Indigenous women. Furthermore, experiencing racism is itself a traumatizing experience that leads to adverse health outcomes such as anxiety, depression, and PTSD.

These factors create serious mental health challenges for people of color, particularly Black people. However, there are now numerous mental health initiatives dedicated to

---

[24] Office of the Surgeon General, Center for Mental Health Services, National Institute of Mental Health, *Mental Health: Culture, Race, and Ethnicity; A Supplement to Mental Health: A Report of the Surgeon General* (Rockville, MD: Substance Abuse and Mental Health Services Administration, 2001), www.ncbi.nlm.nih.gov/books/NBK44243.

bridging this access gap, including the Black Emotional and Mental Health Collective (BEAM), Therapy for Black Girls, and Melanin and Mental Health.[25] If you or a fellow congregant is in need of such services, you can search for national initiatives or ones local to your area.

Access to mental health services is also influenced by financial, geographic, and personal factors. These difficulties in getting care are ripe for public engagement; a congregation's social justice team could consider taking them on.

Mental health activists have worked for decades to challenge a purely medical model of mental health care, maintaining that it fails to deal with the whole person. In particular, it has been a struggle to get public mental health systems to accept that spirituality is an important component in recovery. In recent years, many have acknowledged this; SAMHSA, for instance, includes spirituality as one of its eight dimensions of wellness. We owe a lot to the activists who worked to help make this change possible.

A congregation can get engaged in social justice issues that affect people with mental illness. Unitarian Universalist author and activist Larry Hayes suggests many ways to do this in his excellent book *Mental Illness and Your Town* (see appendix C), and some of his suggestions are included below. One very useful thing congregation members can do is to compile a referral list of reputable local service

---

[25] NAMI, "Identity and Cultural Dimensions: Black/African American," https://www.nami.org/Support-Education/Diverse-Communities/African -American-Mental-Health

providers and advocacy organizations, noting which may welcome volunteers. They might suggest that their congregation formally support community groups working in mental health. It is also very helpful to do a "power study"—a study of who in the community has the power to make decisions that affect the lives of people with mental illness. Such a study can help guide involvement in any of the areas below.

Economic Justice

- **Employment.** Many people with mental illness are unemployed. You might start by working with mental health social workers in your community, who are often charged with finding employment opportunities for their clients. They will be in a good position to know how you can help.
- **Benefits.** Many people with mental illness are dependent on public assistance; when benefits are cut, they may face severe difficulty. Your congregation can connect with the public mental health system so as to know when a budget cut is being proposed and protest it. If cuts are made, the congregation can help members who are affected search for other resources.
- **Transportation.** Many people with mental illness rely on public transportation. They may have to spend several hours a day, on multiple bus routes, to accomplish what a person with a car can do in a matter of

minutes. When bus routes are changed, people can find their lives in disarray. You can research transportation options, and congregations can protest changes that will increase people's struggles.

Abuse Prevention and Response

- **Sexual abuse.** Many people with mental health problems have been sexually abused or raped. Sometimes this has contributed to their mental difficulties. The congregation can research local services for people who have been sexually abused.
- **Institutional abuse.** It is not uncommon for people with mental illness to be abused, physically or sexually, in institutions. If you learn that this has happened to someone, you can help the person to make a formal report and advocate for them with the institution and police.
- **Bullying.** Bullying often contributes to the development of mental health problems. You can look for anti-bullying programs in your community and advocate for their creation if there are none.

Support and Treatment

- **Independent living.** You can research what support is available in your community for people with mental illness to live independently and provide this information to them and their family members. If such support is inadequate, you can advocate for or help provide more.

- **Clubhouse.** Clubhouse International (clubhouse-intl .org) offers people living with mental illness opportunities for friendship, employment, housing, education, and access to medical and psychiatric services in a caring and safe environment. Clubhouse members are valued participants in the work and life of the community, getting support and sharing successes. There are more than three hundred Clubhouses in countries around the world.

- **Addiction.** Appendix C offers some resources and programs for people who have both mental health problems and addictions. Your congregation can research what is available in your community and how to improve the situation.

Mental Health System Involvement and Reform

- **Mental health boards.** Many counties have mental health boards, on which committed members of the community can serve. Mental health boards typically oversee mental health activities in the county and report and make recommendations to the county board of supervisors.

- **Police training.** It is important for police officers to be trained in crisis intervention, such as through the programs offered by CIT International (www.cit international.org). If police are called to intervene when someone is having a mental health crisis, this training greatly reduces the chance of a tragic outcome.
- **Divestment.** Policing currently encompasses a significant part of many city and state budgets. Reallocating money from police forces to often underfunded community programs such as housing, employment, and education can help address the root cause of many mental health disparities, which often stem from instability and trauma.
- **Incarceration.** People with mental illness make up a significant percentage of the inmate population in jails and prisons. If your jurisdiction does not have a mental health court that diverts mentally ill people to treatment rather than incarceration, you can advocate for one to be created.

Publicity

- **News media.** You can urge newspapers, websites, podcasts, and other news sources to spread helpful stories about mental illness or to publish editorials about current issues relating to mental health. You can also write letters to the editor about mental health issues or when the paper has done an especially good or bad job covering them.

- **Individual.** You can work to dispel myths about mental illness and to disseminate information about patients' rights.

Direct Service

- **Volunteering.** You can look for local organizations that welcome volunteers, such as a chapter of the National Alliance on Mental Illness. Hotlines often welcome volunteers and provide training. You could also work with Sidewalk Talk or sponsor outings for people with mental illness, such as to a park, museum, or event.
- **Fundraising.** Members of your congregation could participate in a fundraising walk or hold a benefit event for a mental health organization. Your congregation could also make a direct contribution.

Organized Activism

- **Interfaith work.** Ally with other religious organizations to work for better mental health services and to support each other's members who are struggling with mental health challenges.
- **Community work.** Offer training to enable community leaders to become activists on these issues.

Taking our efforts from the congregation into the community is part of our Unitarian Universalist heritage. The techniques I learned for supporting mental health in the congregation—human kindness, presence, authenticity, acceptance, creating a safer space, and allowing spiritual truths to emerge—have served me well beyond the building's walls. So may it be that we bring all of these lessons with us into the outside world. In so doing, we can help change the world.

—————————— DISCUSSION QUESTIONS ——————————

1. What do you think of the practice of setting up a chair on the sidewalk and offering to listen to anyone who walks by about anything they want to talk about? Is this something that you could do?

2. Why do you think people will talk to strangers about the struggles in their lives when sometimes they don't talk to their own friends or family?

3. Do you think that the Sidewalk Talk practice embodies the elements of good mental health practice outside of the congregation? How so, or how not?

4. What do you think about the different ways to get involved in mental health issues in the community? Which ones might your congregation pursue? Which might you pursue as an individual?

STUDY GUIDE

THIS BOOK can be studied in a congregational context using a format similar to that of covenant groups and allowing for cross-talk. Each session focuses on a different chapter, using the discussion questions that follow it. Allow about ninety minutes for each session. When discussing in a group, remember not to share names or identifying details unless the person you are thinking of has explicitly given you permission to do so in this setting.

Overall session structure

ELEMENT	DESCRIPTION
Opening words and chalice lighting	Suggested opening words: *"Even when our hearts are broken by our own failure or the failure of others cutting into our lives,* *even when we have done all we can and life is still broken,* *there is a Universal Love that has never broken faith with us and never will."* — Rebecca Ann Parker, #184 in *Lifting Our Voices: Readings in the Living Tradition* (Boston: Unitarian Universalist Association, 2015)
Check-in (optional)	If you think you will have enough time, you can ask each person what they are bringing into the meeting.
Silent reflection	
Reading	Select a 3- to 4-page passage from the chapter to read. For short chapters such as the introduction, this may include the entire chapter. For longer ones, choose from the beginning text or one of the subheadings.
Discussion	Use the discussion questions that follow each chapter.

ELEMENT	DESCRIPTION
Check-out	Ask the group, "What will you bring with you from this meeting?" Invite each person to express thanks for specific things they heard or learned.
Closing words	Suggested closing words: *"Take courage, friends.* *The way is often hard, the path is never clear, and the stakes are very high.* *Take courage.* *For deep down, there is another truth:* *you are not alone."* —Wayne Arnason, #698 in *Singing the Living Tradition* (Boston: Beacon Press, 1993)

Appendix B

COMMUNICATION GUIDELINES

SOME PEOPLE find it difficult to speak with someone who has a mental health problem. Sometimes we can understand them, and sometimes not. They may have a perspective that we don't agree with. Rather than arguing with them, we can assume that they have their reasons for what they are doing. Listen to the person and remember that their feelings are real, even if they are not based on reality. Doing so helps preserve interpersonal, family, and congregational harmony. Here are some guidelines for communication with people whose mental disorders may make speaking with them difficult, adapted from advice offered by the National Alliance on Mental Illness. Not all people with mental disorders will have these problems, but when they do, these guidelines will help you connect with them.

WHEN A MENTALLY ILL PERSON...	YOU NEED TO...
has trouble with "reality"	be simple and truthful
is fearful	stay calm
is insecure	be accepting
has trouble concentrating	be brief, repeat yourself, clarify what you are hearing
is overstimulated	limit input, not force discussion
is easily agitated	recognize their agitation, allow them to take a break for a while if they need to
has poor judgment	not expect rational discussion
is preoccupied	get their attention first
is withdrawn	initiate relevant conversation
has little empathy for you	recognize this as a symptom
believes delusions	empathize without arguing
has low self-esteem and little motivation	stay positive
is in crisis, speaking loudly and fast	match the person's speaking volume and rate, then slowly reduce your own. This will encourage the other person to do the same.

Make positive requests in a direct, pleasant, and honest way:

1. Look at the person.
2. Say exactly what you would like the person to do.
3. Say how their doing it would make you feel.

Example: "I would like you to dry the dishes. That would help me and brighten my day."

Express negative feelings in an effective, nonthreatening way:

1. Look at the person.
2. Say exactly and firmly what the person did to upset you and how their doing it made you feel.
3. Suggest what you would like them to do differently in the future.

Example: "I feel angry that you shouted at me. I'd like it if you spoke quieter next time."

Use praise and warm encouragement to cheer on any progress, no matter how small, while ignoring flaws. Be specific. These can be in the form of attention, physical affection, expressions of interest, or commendation.

Avoid negative and disheartening remarks. Research shows that people are at greater risk of relapse when they often hear

- blaming,
- threats,
- highly emotional responses,
- negative stereotypes,
- denigrations of their character,
- minimization of their distress,
- advice to "buck up," or
- too many demands on them or arbitrary limits on their behaviors.

These communication guidelines are not something you will resort to just once. People with mental disorders need connection and encouragement all the time, and sometimes they need to be reminded that you love and care for them over and over again. Even when they fail. Especially when they fail.

RESOURCES

Caring for People with Mental Health Issues

The **Unitarian Universalist Mental Health Network** (uumentalhealth.org) promotes the inclusion of people affected by mental health issues both in our congregations and in society at large. It offers a wide variety of resources and describes many other websites, books, and movies about mental health. Of particular interest on the UUMHN's website are

- The **Caring Congregation Curriculum** (uumental health.org/education/the-caring-congregation -curriculum), offering a seven-workshop series teaching congregations how to welcome and support people with mental health difficulties. Also available are an abbreviated two-workshop version of the curriculum, a four-workshop series designed for children, and a two-workshop series to train pastoral care workers. One effective approach for a congregation to take is to first train the pastoral care team and then offer education to the whole congregation.

- My own *Mental Health Information for Ministers and Lay Leaders* (uumentalhealth.org/wp-content/uploads/2018/12/Mental-Health-Webinar-Handout.pdf), a guide on how to handle mental health challenges in congregations.

The mental health ministry I lead at Mission Peak Unitarian Universalist Congregation, Fremont, California (mpuuc.org/mhm), offers a variety of resources, including

- a collection of sermons on mental health by me and others
- information about how to arrange for me to teach a workshop or webinar
- more than sixty episodes of *Mental Health Matters TV*, a public-access show produced by Shannon Eliot and me. Two episodes focus on spirituality.
- sixteen videos of people telling their recovery stories, plus links to similar videos hosted elsewhere

Pathways to Promise (www.pathways2promise.org) offers liturgical and educational materials, program models, and networking information to clergy and lay leaders of all faiths, to promote a caring ministry with people with mental illness and their families. Together with the Seattle-based **Mental Health Chaplaincy** (www.mentalhealthchaplaincy .org), Pathways to Promise administers the **Companionship Movement** (www.thecompanionshipmovement.org), a practice of presence that supports healing and recovery through community.

Mental Health Ministries (www.mentalhealthministries .net) is an interfaith web-based ministry that provides educational resources to help erase the stigma of mental illness in our faith communities. Mental Health Ministries offers a wide variety of print and media resources, with many of the print resources also available in Spanish. The website also has training curricula and other resources developed by denominations and national groups working in the areas of spirituality/ faith and mental illness.

The United Church of Christ's Mental Health Network (mhn-ucc.blogspot.com) works to reduce stigma and promote the inclusion of people with mental illness and brain disorders and their families in the life, leadership, and work of congregations.

Sally Patton's book, *Welcoming Children with Special Needs: A Guidebook for Faith Communities* (Boston: Unitarian Universalist Association, 2004) is the best resource available on including and supporting children with mental health problems in congregations. It is available free on the UUA's website at www.uua.org/children.

Faith. Hope. Life. (actionallianceforsuicideprevention.org/faithhopelife) has an excellent collection of suicide prevention resources for ministers and faith communities.

The **National Alliance on Mental Illness** (www.nami.org) is a grassroots mental health organization that does advocacy, education, support, and public awareness work to help individuals and families affected by mental illness build better lives. Among many other resources, it offers

- Family-to-Family, a free eight-session course for family, significant others, and friends of people with mental health conditions. This course is available in both English and Spanish.
- Peer-to-Peer, a free eight-session course for adults with mental health conditions who are looking to better understand themselves and their recovery.
- Basics, a free six-session course specifically for those caring for youth experiencing mental health problems.
- FaithNet NAMI, an interfaith network that aims to educate and inspire faith communities about mental illness and the vital role spirituality plays in many people's recovery.

The **National Empowerment Center** (www.power2u.org) brings a message of recovery, empowerment, hope, and healing to people who have experienced mental health issues, trauma, or extreme states. The organization is run by and for consumers, survivors, and ex-patients of the mental health system.

The **Substance Abuse and Mental Health Services Administration** (www.samhsa.gov/recovery) is the agency within the United States Department of Health and Human Services that leads public health efforts to advance the behavioral health of the nation and reduce the impact of substance abuse and mental illness on America's communities. The website offers a great deal of information on mental health recovery, guides to finding treatment, and helplines, as well as free webinars that discuss various aspects of recovery from mental illness and substance abuse.

Emotional CPR (www.emotional-cpr.org) is an educational program designed to teach people to assist others through an emotional crisis. It is based on three simple steps: connecting with the person in crisis, empowering them, and revitalizing their relationships with loved ones and support systems.

The **Wellness Recovery Action Plan** (WRAP; mentalhealth recovery.com) is a self-designed prevention and wellness process that anyone can use. It guides people to develop their own wellness tools, identify warning signs of crisis, and develop plans for what to do during and after a crisis. It is now used extensively by people in all kinds of circumstances and by health care and mental health systems all over the world to address a variety of physical health, mental health, and life issues.

Mental Health First Aid (www.mentalhealthfirstaid.org) is a skill-based training course that teaches participants how to assist someone having a mental health or substance use–related crisis. As well as courses aimed generally at adults and at teens, there are specialized curricula for such groups as veterans, firefighters and EMS personnel, and many others.

Problematic Behavior and Congregational Safety

The UUA's **Safe Congregations** website (www.uua.org/safe) offers guidance on a wide variety of topics, including many that may result from mental health issues in a congregation. It suggests ways to develop behavioral covenants and covenants of right relations, policies on disruptive behavior, and appropriate ways of managing conflict.

Kenneth C. Haugk, *Antagonists in the Church: How to Identify and Deal with Destructive Conflict* (Minneapolis, MN: Augsburg Publishing House, 1988).

Wayne E. Oates, *The Care of Troublesome People* (New York: Alban Institute, 1994).

Wayne E. Oates, *Behind the Masks: Personality Disorders in Religious Behavior* (Philadelphia: The Westminster Press, 1987).

Marshall Shelley, *Well-Intentioned Dragons: Ministering to Problem People in the Church* (Minneapolis, MN: Bethany House Publishers, 1985).

Paul T. Mason and Randi Kreger, *Stop Walking on Eggshells: Taking Your Life Back When Someone You Care About Has Borderline Personality Disorder,* second edition (Oakland, CA: New Harbinger Publications, 2010).

Robert M. Bramson, *Coping with Difficult People* (New York: Ballantine, 1984).

Social Action: Empowering and Defending the Rights of People with Mental Illness

Larry Hayes, *Mental Illness and Your Town: 37 Ways for Communities to Help and Heal* (Ann Arbor, MI: Loving Healing Press, 2009).

MindFreedom International (www.mindfreedom.org) is a nonprofit organization that unites sponsor and affiliate grassroots groups with thousands of individual members to win human rights and alternatives to conventional medical mental health care for people labeled with psychiatric disabilities.

The **National Coalition for Disability Rights** (www.ndrn .org) offers training and technical assistance to legal advocacy networks and advocates for laws protecting the civil and human rights of all people with disabilities.

Addiction-Specific Resources

The **Unitarian Universalist Addictions Ministry** (uuaddictions ministry.org) works to educate individuals, families, congregations, and communities about addiction and recovery. Among the many resources it offers is an information sheet on co-occurring psychiatric disorders.

See information in the previous section on the **Substance Abuse and Mental Health Services Administration** (www .samhsa.gov/recovery), which covers both mental health and substance abuse.

Denis Meacham, *The Addiction Ministry Handbook: A Guide for Faith Communities* (Boston: Skinner House Books, 2004).

Ken and Cathlean, eds., *Twelve-Step Unitarian Universalists: Essays on Recovery* (Boston: Skinner House Books, 2014).

Calendar Observances

Congregations may wish to mark one or more of these nationally designated observances:

- May is **Mental Health Awareness Month**, originally established in 1949 by Mental Health America (www .mhanational.org).
- September is **National Recovery Month**, sponsored by the Substance Abuse and Mental Health Services Administration (www.recoverymonth.gov).
- The first full week of October is **Mental Illness Awareness Week**, established by Congress in 1990 in recognition of the work of the National Alliance on Mental Illness (www.nami.org).

ACKNOWLEDGMENTS

I OFFER MY THANKS to Mary Benard, my editor at Skinner House Books, for suggesting I write the book, and to Mary, the developmental editor Steven Scipione, copyeditor Shoshanna Green, and other reviewers for giving excellent feedback and suggestions. I am grateful for suggestions from reviewers of early drafts: Rev. Mark Belletini, Rev. John Buehrens, Dr. Daniel Fisher, Janet Holden, Sr. Nancy Kehoe, Jay Mahler, and Rev. Kathleen Rolenz.

I thank Rev. Mark Belletini, who is the first Unitarian Universalist minister I ever knew, for supporting me in my first steps of recovery at Starr King Unitarian Universalist Church in Hayward, California. I am also grateful to the members of that church who, by living their faith, helped to heal me.

Starr King School for the Ministry taught me to be spiritually authentic and supported my ministerial formation in an unusual community ministry.

I also acknowledge the important contributions of a number of other people:

- Dr. Bruce Fabric, my wise psychiatrist since 1978, who saved my life and who introduced me to the importance of spirituality in recovery.
- Rev. Jeffrey Spencer, my spiritual director, who has supported my spiritual development for nearly a decade.
- Members of my Community Ministry Advisory Committee, who meet with me on a quarterly basis:
  - James "Scotty" Scott, director of the Life Reaching Across to Life peer support mental health center and my supervisor there.
  - Peggy Rahman, president of the Alameda County chapter of the National Alliance on Mental Illness (NAMI) and an early ally within my church community on mental health issues.
  - Dr. Charles Reed, a talented and wise psychologist in the Fremont, California, area.
  - Dr. Elizabeth Maynard Schaefer, author of *Writing through the Darkness*, a book on how creative writing can help depression, and a dedicated congregation member.
- The members of Mission Peak Unitarian Universalist Congregation in Fremont, who have honored and supported me in discerning my call to ministry and have helped me answer it.

- The clients of Reaching Across, who are my heroes and teachers every day.

And most of all, I thank my dear husband, Tom Meyers, and my daughter, Carol, and her family, for being my anchors and my supports for many decades, through all the twists and turns that my life has taken.

ABOUT THE AUTHOR

Rev. Barbara F. Meyers is a Unitarian Universalist community minister, affiliated with Mission Peak Unitarian Universalist Congregation in Fremont, California, whose ministry focuses on mental health issues. She works as assistant director of Life Reaching Across to Life, a peer-support mental health center in Fremont. In the course of her ministry she has, among other projects, written a mental health curriculum for congregations, produced a mental health public access TV show, helped start a counseling center, and founded a community listening project affiliated with Sidewalk Talk (www.sidewalk-talk.org). Denominationally, she has been involved in the leadership of EqUUal Access (www.equual access.org), an organization of Unitarian Universalists living with disabilities and their allies that promotes the full engagement of people with disabilities in UU communities and the broader society, since its founding in 2008. She also helped establish the Accessibility and Inclusion Ministry congregational certification program (www.equualaccess.org/ aim-program) in 2015, a program that she now helps to direct, and the Unitarian Universalist Mental Health Network, where she serves as president of the board.

She has a BA in mathematics and an MS and PhD in computer science, all from UCLA, and worked for IBM for twenty-five years as a software engineer before moving into ministry. She received a master of divinity degree from Starr King School for the Ministry in 2004 and a certificate in spiritual direction from the Chaplaincy Institute in 2011. Her work for mental health has been recognized with awards from her county and the State of California.

Besides mental health, her interests and spiritual practices are weaving, sewing, playing piano, running, reading, and playing with her grandsons.